Copping Out

COPPING OUT

The Consequences of Police Corruption and Misconduct

Anthony Stanford
Foreword by Brian S. Bentley

 PRAEGER

AN IMPRINT OF ABC-CLIO, LLC
Santa Barbara, California • Denver, Colorado • Oxford, England

Library of Congress Cataloging-in-Publication Data
Stanford, Anthony.
    Copping out : the consequences of police corruption and misconduct / Anthony Stanford ; foreword by Brian S. Bentley.
       pages cm
    Includes bibliographical references and index.
    ISBN 978–1–4408–3089–1 (hard copy : alk. paper) — ISBN 978–1–4408–3090–7 (ebook) 1. Police corruption—United States. 2. Police misconduct—United States. 3. Police—United States. I. Title.
HV7936.C85S697   2015
364.1'3230973—dc23   2014040772

ISBN: 978–1–4408–3089–1
EISBN: 978–1–4408–3090–7

19 18 17 16 15   1 2 3 4 5

This book is also available on the World Wide Web as an eBook.
Visit www.abc-clio.com for details.

Praeger
An Imprint of ABC-CLIO, LLC

ABC-CLIO, LLC
130 Cremona Drive, P.O. Box 1911
Santa Barbara, California 93116-1911

This book is printed on acid-free paper ∞

Manufactured in the United States of America

To my siblings, James Jr., Larry, Toi, Linda, Robbie, Angel, Harold, and Margaret: consider, against the odds, what we have accomplished.

Contents

Foreword

I am living testament that police brutality and corruption is alive and manifesting in urban America. As a Los Angeles Police officer assigned to South Central Los Angeles, I witnessed and partook in brutal arrests that made the beating of the late Rodney King look like grade-school love taps. I relished the power and authority of my badge and gun, seizing every opportunity I could to flex it.

"You can't do that!" they always screamed in desperation. "I know my rights!"

Knowing your civil rights and being able to protect them are two different things. As a police officer, I never came across anyone who could protect the rights granted to them by the U.S. Constitution, especially under the cover of darkness and the concealment of a back alley.

Most people are under the impression they are fighting against incompetent and uneducated police officers, since a GED is all that is required to become a law enforcement officer in most municipalities. Police officers are trained to circumvent civil rights with the precision of brain surgeons. I was taught that every good police officer could find probable cause or reasonable suspicion to detain anyone, especially a black man. In roll call, I was provided with crime statistics and enough general suspect descriptions to stop any black man I chose. A community leader or civil rights activist never influenced my actions in any way. I pretty much did what I wanted because I was thoroughly trained in how to justify it. Besides, I never knew any police officer who had been fired or suspended because of a press conference by a community leader or civil rights activist.

When a victim of racial profiling or corruption takes on a legal battle with a local police department, they are fighting against the entire city and all of its resources, which include city attorneys whose job is to protect the city from financial loss. The investigation always begins with the complainant. Your life better be in order, especially for police officers who speak out against their department.

I bucked the system by writing a tell-all book about the culture of violence within the Los Angeles Police Department and became the subject of an administrative lynching. The Los Angeles Police Department tried to smear my name and reputation by charging me with false allegations of misconduct. I was lashed and beaten to a pulp by the department's disciplinary system until I was unjustly terminated. Other police officers who also spoke out and somehow managed to survive were metaphorically castrated and their careers left for dead. They were demoralized and doomed to a stagnant career behind a desk.

Remove all law enforcement officers and start over. Within three years, the same problems of corruption and brutality will arise again. Corruption and police brutality is the nature of the business. I worked with four partners who were arrested, convicted, and sentenced to prison for various felony crimes including two for rape, one for bank robbery, and another for heading an auto theft ring. All of them were idealist cadets and believed they could change the world by becoming police officers. They were wrong. The job changed them for the worse.

Copping Out: The Consequences of Police Corruption and Misconduct is the early beam of light that uncovers and exposes one of America's darkest secrets. That secret is the police brutality and corruption that many Americans refuse to acknowledge. Abusive cops, like the mythical boogie man, are rarely seen by the general public, and their destruction and carnage is usually explained away by diffusive terms like gang member, thug, or ex-convict.

I was intrigued when I learned that Anthony Stanford had written a book about police brutality and corruption because the topic is essential to the preservation of those who "fit the description." Believe me when I say Stanford's book is on point. I agree with him when he says, "Power cannot be absolute. We must have checks and balances." I believe him when he says, "Power tends to corrupt."

Stanford needs to be commended for his work. I highly recommend *Copping Out: The Consequences of Police Corruption and Misconduct.* It is a great resource for people who want to research brutality and corruption issues. Anthony Stanford's examples are concrete, his referen-ces are extremely credible, and the subject matter is relevant as civil unrest becomes increasingly volatile and turbulent as it did in the 1960s. Upon completion of this book, readers will be able to engage in a more informa-tive dialogue about police brutality and corruption. It is my hope that the frightening and disturbing truth will help us form a viable plan of action.

Brian S. Bentley, former officer,
Los Angeles Police Department

Acknowledgments

I am grateful to Beth Goins for indexing my third book. I would also like to thank Brian S. Bentley for penning a foreword that introduces this book in a unique and heartfelt way. A special thanks to Aurora's chief of police Gregory S. Thomas for allowing members of his command to contribute their professional and personal opinions to an issue that is so very important to forging a collaborative relationship between police officers and citizens nationwide. Finally, thank you to my lifelong friend Sonia Irwin, whose personal journey continues to transform lives.

1

Copping Out: An Introduction

On a rainy spring morning in 1965, my mother and I watched from the living room window as six white Chicago Police officers viciously pummeled a young black man. The individual appeared to be no more than 18 years old and was beaten with nightsticks, kicked, and pounded by the police even as he lay helpless on the rain-soaked walkway. Like us, neighbors that witnessed the beating were horrified, and in the days and weeks ahead, the conversation about what had occurred turned to what should be done about it, if anything. I recall that some of the adults wanted to call the police, while others believed that it would not make a difference since the police had been involved. Though many witnessed the incident from start to finish, there was never any confirmation of what precipitated the beating and arrest, or if an investigation into the incident was ever conducted. Still, a half century later, the indelible memory of the relentless thud of the nightsticks striking the young man's body and that of the red-faced police officers standing over him as he lay on the pavement, his blood mixing with the soaking rain, is one of my earliest memories of Chicago's finest, those sworn to serve and protect.

For all any of us knew, the individual taken into custody that morning might have posed an imminent danger to the community or to the police officers that subdued and arrested him. It was also entirely possible that the officers had no choice other than to level the severe beating, in order to restrain the individual and to prevent the situation from spiraling further out of control. However, from my point of view after more than

50 years, my gut tells me that, in this instance, to give the officers involved in the incident the benefit of the doubt would be to dismiss what I witnessed. The difficulty in explaining away what I saw with my own eyes that morning is likely attributed to the fact that it was about this time that my consciousness related to race, the civil rights movement, and the reality of white dominion was taking shape. What I remember clearly is the confusion I experienced seeing police officers behave in this manner. Recalling the incident opens a window to contemporary society, where incidents like that of a half-century ago, and worse, are commonplace. While not entirely, the vicious beating is among the reasons that I decided to write this book. Yet, the dissemination of information related to the growing divide between law enforcement on one hand and the minority and economically disadvantaged on the other, throughout urban America, is the primary reason.

I am convinced that the gravity of a beating leveled by the police, at least from my perspective as a black child, can be the genesis of the complicated relationship that African Americans have with members of law enforcement. In the mind's eye of an impressionable young person, it can become a lasting example and explain how the "us against them" relationship begins for countless minority children in urban America. In spite of the fact that while growing up, the father of my best friend was an African American police officer and two white neighbors held leadership positions on the Chicago Police Department (CPD) and were role models in the community, after witnessing the beating, something began to change. That said, I was utterly confused and found it enormously difficult to fathom that the police officers that I had seen day in, day out, coming and going, would participate in the brutal beating of another human being, absent an immediate peril to their lives, or the lives of others.

At some point, it crossed my mind that every black man that I've ever had a serious discussion with about the treatment of minorities by the police has been shaded by a bad experience, or marked some incident, at which they realized that the snappy uniform, badge, and sidearm were only symbols intended to influence the mindset of the public and to keep them in line. In nearly every instance, many have told me that they eventually had to reckon with the realities that changed their perspective about police, the criminal justice system, and how both viewed them. This is not to say that because of this, recognition of the immense responsibility of police officers is undervalued, or their authority dismissed. However, they have in common the awareness that possessing police power does not automatically equate to a sense of fairness, nor should it be deemed as proof of one's character or integrity, and definitely not an indication of their sense of humanity.

Reinforced by personal experience, the lesson is often learned under hostile circumstances that are difficult to imagine and, for some non-minorities, impossible to accept. Yet time and again, truth has a way of ultimately transforming a once idealistic perception of police officers and the criminal justice system, from one of admiration and respect to one that must take into account that young black men, in particular, must develop a skillset in order to survive in an urban environment plagued by gangs, guns, crime, and a hostile police presence. Make no mistake that reconciling this reality provoked by racial, social, and economic overtones is one of great concern and urgency.

A half-century ago, long before the advent of social media and cell-phone cameras and the ability to record negative encounters with law enforcement, such incidents were far less talked about and generally swept under the rug. Because of the ability to command, contain, and control without the specter of cable news or TMZ, police were not widely seen as having an adversarial relationship with minorities and economically disadvantaged people. With the exception of what was going on, beyond the Mason-Dixon Line, generally in white America, police officers—and, for that matter, the entire criminal justice system—were known for their heroic deeds, deterring the criminal element, and being essential to maintaining law and order. At the same time, adverse encounters with minorities were commonplace and had for many years prevented the trusting relationship that is commonly shared by whites as it relates to law enforcement and the criminal justice system. Among minorities, ambivalence and outright distrust of police officers and the criminal justice system, especially in black communities, is the norm. Needless to say, when rumors of police wrongdoing and atrocious criminal and disturbing acts against the very people that they are sworn and paid to serve and protect are substantiated, police officers become indistinguishable from the bad guys. When this occurs, it reinforces the unsettling misconception that all police officers and, some believe, the entire American criminal justice system is tainted, rigged, biased, and morally corrupt.

Moreover, in exceedingly egregious cases in which evidence of police brutality, misconduct, and criminal behavior is divulged and subsequently proven to be factual, it serves to some as confirmation that the true function of law enforcement is to suppress the downtrodden and to wreak havoc on minority communities, with the intended purpose of keeping them under control. As a matter of fact, many minorities, especially those that reside in predominately black neighborhoods, distrust law enforcement and the entire criminal justice system. Indeed, early on, they adopt the code of silence known in the black community as "no snitching." It is a sentiment that is increasingly pervasive, and one that poses a great challenge to police officers and law enforcement hierarchies nationwide. Compounding the problem is that the negative opinion of police and our system of justice in general is being passed from generation to generation.

I know that my personal sensitivities regarding the role and presence of the police in the black community began to dramatically change several years after witnessing the young man's brutal beating. My eyes were open to the potential menace behind the facade that some had warned existed, and they had validated through personal encounters with law enforcement. The 1965 incident had been my first glimpse of what had been unthinkable. The affect that race and economic status brought, as it relates to one's experience with the police and criminal justice system, introduced a level of concern that would play out several years later.

Apart from the time that my friend and I were lighting firecrackers in the alley directly behind my home, and that instead of taking us to our parents, white officers took us to the police station and placed us in an actual cell, I consider what I experienced on December 4, 1969, as my first substantial encounter with CPD officers. The firecracker incident could have been to teach us a lesson. However, what occurred nearly a half-century ago could not be mistaken for anything other than unprovoked racism and hostility aimed at blacks. What occurred in the predawn hours on a cold December morning still ranks among Chicago's most racially motivated incidents involving members of law enforcement. It played out in an impoverished black community on the West Side of Chicago, and it was here that the stories I had been told over my young life collided with my recollection of the young man being brutally beaten several years earlier, changing forever the way that I viewed police and the American criminal justice system.

It happened when I was with my father, an independent merchant, delivering artificial Christmas trees on the West Side. My father had once owned a tavern, but he had turned to working as a street vendor, providing for his family by selling an assortment of merchandise from an oversized cargo van. From eight-track tapes to women's fashions, his innate knack for knowing what people needed, or wanted, before they realized it was an attribute that complemented his survival skillset. His many years of hard work moved us into Chicago's emerging black middle class.

Dad had routinely sold his goods all over Chicago. However, he had not ventured to the West Side since the assassination of Dr. Martin Luther

King. As in several other American cities, after Dr. King was killed by a sniper's bullet in 1968, riots devastated West Madison Street, a Chicago major business district frequented by blacks. Following the murder of the civil rights icon, incensed blacks who were fed up with abject poverty, demoralized, and hopeless, burned block after block of what had been a thriving area for small businesses and independent merchants. The rioting, torching of buildings, and looting is believed to have worsened conditions for an already oppressed black community. Moreover, the disorder and mob action backfired, creating losses for the proprietors of brick-and-mortar businesses, and also street merchants like my father, resulting in economic hardship. The 1968 riots would ultimately trigger high unemployment, gang activity, and urban blight that lasted for decades.

After months of absence from the riot-ravaged West Side, my father planned to return there and resume hawking goods to people that he considered loyal customers. I desperately wanted to go along and to see what had been described on network news as utter and senseless destruction. So, in the weeks prior to my father's return, I petitioned my parents to allow me to skip school, convincing them that it would be a unique learning experience.

There was absolutely nothing about the December morning to indicate that on this day, the vestiges of my youthful idealism would give way to the reality of racial inequality and indifference. It had not entered my mind that within the hour, I would see clearly what the priorities for black people, especially black males, were required to be in order to navigate and survive in a world where some preferred their extinction. For the first time in my life, I became acutely aware of a truth that was exceedingly difficult to understand, yet necessary to accept. As events unfolded that morning, I can't say that I was entirely conscious of what it all meant, or that I understood that what had been a period of black optimism and ethnic pride was coming to an end. However, I am certain that if I had the same decision to make today, I would still choose to accompany my father.

As we made our way to the first delivery, I thought about what I had heard a neighbor say to my father about the 1968 riots and the destruction of the West Side business district. I recall that the man seemed agitated as he talked about the disastrous events that occurred over several days, as buildings were set afire by angry blacks. What I remember most is that the intensity of his anger was matched by a palpable anxiety as he described the destruction. "What they did is a damn shame and disgrace," the man said as though he was distancing himself from not only the rioting, but also the black race. In his anger he was not alone, because the riots had also moved Chicago mayor Richard J. Daley to make extreme statements—for example, amid the riots, issuing his infamous, "shoot to kill order."

Unbeknownst to us, before dawn that morning, arguably the most powerful national black movement in American history edged closer toward obliteration from the political and social landscape. In an explosion of what is believed to have been controlled chaos and gunfire, a confrontation between police and the Illinois chapter of the Black Panthers ratcheted up racial tension, ushering in an era of profound distrust of police officers and the entire criminal justice system. Nearly half a century later, the consequence of what occurred continues to haunt the black psyche. Despite prolific gains, including the election of Barack Obama as America's first black president, inside black urban America, the byproducts of suspicion, animosity, and disregard toward police and the whole criminal justice system prevails.

When we exited the expressway, in every direction, there were police. They were in squad cars and on motorcycles, and plainclothes detectives were milling about. As we inched toward the intersection where a husky white police officer directed traffic, I saw a look of concern on my father's face. Once there, my father lowered the window and politely asked, "Officer, what's going on?" To which the police officer barked, "Don't worry about it—just get your black ass out of here!" I had never heard anyone speak to my father in this way, and I was overcome with anger. To this day, I don't understand why, but there were what seemed like several minutes of silence. Not only that, but I avoided making eye contact with my father, yet I distinctly remember that his anger and humiliation were intense. I could sense the anger from the sound of his breathing and, from my peripheral vision, could see that he was struggling to somehow cope with the rage and embarrassment that he felt.

Several minutes later, we learned that Chicago police officers had killed two Black Panthers in an early morning shootout. Chicago radio reported that the charismatic Illinois Black Panther chairman Fred Hampton and its defense minister Mark Clark had been killed in a shootout a few hours earlier. In the months following the deaths of Hampton and Clark, it was revealed that more than 100 bullets had been fired by Chicago police officers during the early morning attack on the Black Panther's headquarters. Moreover, independent ballistic tests performed by the FBI confirmed that the Black Panthers had fired just one bullet. Needless to say, we were shocked to discover that the shootout had occurred next door to our very first customer.

With my father upstairs assembling a Christmas tree, and my arms loaded with boxes of ornaments, a boy in his early teens held the door open for me. As I passed him, in a strong and defiant voice, he said, "those damn pigs killed the Chairman." In response to his intensely powerful words, I managed to say, "Yeah, I know." I still cringe recalling the poignant words of this young person, and how his expression of tremendous loss so magnified my shallowness. Driving away, I saw him again, this time with a clenched fist raised high in the air.

We never returned to the West Side, and the demand for justice in the killing of the Black Panthers would eventually wane. However, not before tremendous protest and demands for an independent investigation and justice for what many continue to believe was the ordered double-murder of the Black Panther leaders, perpetrated by sworn officers of Chicago's law enforcement. Dr. Quentin Young, a white man and member of the political team of Chicago's first black mayor, Harold Washington, would later say this about Fred Hampton: "He (Hampton) was a giant, and this is not some idle white worship of a black man," and "[t]his is a terrible way to put it, but the people who made it their business to kill the leaders of the black movement picked the right ones."[1] I wholeheartedly agree with Dr. Young's daring assessment.

While blaming the entire criminal justice system would be unfair, after more than four decades, there are still those who believe the brazen leadership of the Black Panthers resulted in the deaths of Hampton and Clark. The Black Panthers had begun to address the despair and disgrace that had for generations spread through minority and poor communities. The movement's end, at least in Chicago, culminated in an attack by law enforcement, cutting short the lives of the Black Panther leaders, and in doing so, eliminating the once powerful movement from the social fabric of black urban society. The result is thought to be the glorification of violence, self-degradation, and misogyny. At the same time, a disregard and contempt for law enforcement was flourishing.

I don't intend to suggest that only white police officers commit abusive and criminal acts. Nor should what appears in the following chapters be construed as an indication of how all blacks, minorities, and the economically disadvantaged feel about law enforcement. It stands to reason that law enforcement, like any other profession, is comprised of both good and bad. However, on the South and West Sides of Chicago, during the mid-to-late 1960s and continuing today, there is an overwhelming sentiment held principally in black communities of distrust and cynicism toward the police officers. The reality is that, in some neighborhoods, police officers are perceived as an enemy of the people, much like the gangs that peddle drugs and whose gun violence has become an ethnic-specific epidemic. While some may consider this to be an extreme viewpoint, an increasing number of blacks categorize police officers as hooligans paid with taxpayer dollars to intimidate urban dwellers.

Officers provided with arms and police powers to patrol neighborhoods are believed by many to purposely terrorize citizens, while the officers themselves engage in various nefarious criminal enterprises. Surely this will strike some as being over the top; however, the fact is that there is ample evidence to support the contention. While some may attribute it to a small number of police officers, reports indicate that police hierarchies are genuinely concerned with the increasing number of law enforcement officers that are implicated in police wrongdoing. Still, unfortunately, the actions of some, or even a few, can sully the reputation of police officers everywhere and smear that of the many who take seriously their sworn oath to serve and protect.

Just as there is a long history of glamorizing the American gangster and treating them as celebrities, wayward police officers and their involvement in criminal deeds are, for profit and our entertainment, romanticized by Hollywood. For instance, long before Denzel Washington's chilling Oscar-winning performance as the rouge, sociopathic Los Angeles police detective Alonzo Harris in the 2001 movie *Training Day*, there were real police officers whose infamy and legend exposed the seedy side, hooliganism, and criminal element that has long been a part of law enforcement agencies.

A case in point is the notorious police officer "Two-Gun Pete," who terrorized the streets of Chicago's South Side during the 1930s and 1940s. In his July 21, 2013, *Chicago Tribune* article, reporter William Lee shed light on Sylvester Washington, aka "Two-Gun Pete," an African American Chicago police officer that intimidated the black community from 1934 until leaving the police force in 1951. In the article, Lee talks about Two-Gun Pete, saying that, "Though he was one of the deadliest police officers in Chicago history, few people without a longtime South Side connection have ever heard of Two-Gun Pete or the enigmatic man behind the nickname, Sylvester Washington."[2]

To those who knew him or recall his lengthy and seemingly terror-filled reign tolerated by the CPD hierarchy, Two-Gun Pete was well known for his brutality and is said to have shot down 12 men. Sylvester's former wife Rosalind Washington Banks, who married Sylvester when she was 16 and he 58, described Sylvester saying that, "He was the meanest, cruelest person." Native Chicagoan and 27-time Grammy Award winner Quincy Jones recalled in his autobiography, *Q: The Autobiography of Quincy Jones*, how Two-Gun Pete struck fear into so many South Side residents: "Every weekend we watched a legendary black cop named Two-Gun

Pete who carried two pearl-handled revolvers shoot black kids in the back in broad daylight, right in front of a Walgreens drugstore—the kids dropped like potato sacks ... We fantasized about making Two-Gun Pete pay."[3]

The documented brutality and atrocities of Two-Gun Pete, and that of other corrupt and menacing police officers, more than three-quarters of a century ago signaled that significant change was needed in order to screen and to prevent this sort of individual from entering the law enforcement ranks. Because the measures taken were apparently too little and too late, in contemporary society the problem has been exacerbated. Moreover, besides the fact that the nefarious acts of wayward police are unfairly heaped on the reputation of hard-working men and women in uniform, and that their atrocious behavior has a negative effect on officer morale and the law enforcement profession overall, wrongdoing by police officers is something that law enforcement agencies across the country can't seem to eradicate. Well aware of the potential threat that power, accessibility, and temptation play in the comportment and career of the rank and file, the law enforcement chain of command is attempting to counter the lures that cause some officers to cross the proverbial line.

In addition to the recognizable enticements of access and opportunity, modern-day law enforcement commands must also deal with fairly new challenges—for example, battling against infiltration by street gangs and other villainous elements. Topping the goals that street gangs wish to attain is that of penetrating law enforcement and exploiting, for the purpose of spreading their criminal influence, the use of police powers. The threat posed by street gangs with an official role within law enforcement threatens to weaken the integrity of our system of justice. Besides infringing upon the people's trust in and respect of police officers to patrol and keep our streets safe, it brings about untold dangers.

However, according to some, gangs are attempting to breach not only the traditional systems of government such as law enforcement agencies, the U.S. military, and political organizations. For example, in 2014, the National Football League's Philadelphia Eagles released DeSean Jackson, a star wide receiver with a five-year, $48.5 million contract, for alleged affiliation with gangs. It should be noted that despite the allegations, Jackson was picked up by the Washington Redskins, and he spoke to the claims of gang ties in a statement:

> I would like to address the misleading and unfounded reports that my release has anything to do with any affiliation that has been specu-lated surrounding the company I keep off of the field. I would like

to make it very clear that I am not and never have been part of any gang. I am not a gang member and to speculate and assume that I am involved in such activity off the field is reckless and irresponsible.

I work very hard on and off the field and I am a good person with good values. I am proud of the accomplishments that I have made both on and off the field. I have worked tirelessly to give back to my community and have a positive impact on those in need. It is unfortunate that I now have to defend myself and my intentions.

These reports are irresponsible and just not true. I look forward to working hard for my new team.[4]

Donovan Warren, who grew up with Jackson and also used his athletic ability to enhance his future prospects, summed it up by saying, "We are a product of our environment."[5] It is a contention made by individuals who insist that it should not be compulsory to break all ties with their past simply because of their accomplishments.

Political ambition also plays a major role, as it relates to the way that people perceive the criminal justice system. From the Federal Bureau of Investigation (FBI), to local law enforcement agencies, the issue of law and order is something that hugely affects political ambition. In the chapters that follow, you will see examples of underreacting and overreacting to allegations of police wrongdoing, and the effect that it can have on society. Sometimes driven by ambitious political candidates and prosecutors, efforts to demonstrate zero tolerance for police misconduct can give the appearance of overcompensating for unchecked criminal activity within law enforcement ranks. In fact, there is a fairly strong case to be made that the prosecution of some police officers is directly linked to political ambition. While many are well documented and supported by a need and public demand that something be done, according to *Frontline*, there were as many as 17 active investigations by the Department of Justice (DOJ) into police wrongdoing in 2011. In spite of a flurry of federal investigations and prosecutorial action, the allegations of police wrongdoing have not quelled.[6]

The possibility of police corruption or that of widespread criminal activity from within a law enforcement agency conjures up ominous feelings. It eats away at the public trust and introduces an anxiety that is difficult for the public to overcome, and is something akin to the fear of unknowing. For instance, in March 2014, soon after Malaysia Airlines Flight 370 went missing, the pilot and copilot were considered by law enforcement officials to have intentionally brought down the

Boeing 777 jet. If proven true, it would change the mindset of almost every person who boards an airplane. Suddenly, the long-standing trust afforded as a result of the integrity and professionalism of pilots would be dramatically transformed.

After all is said and done, there are individuals like Police Commander Kristen Ziman, a 23-year veteran of the Aurora Police Department (APD) and the first female police commander for the City of Aurora, Illinois, police department. Aurora, the second-largest city in Illinois, is about 45 miles west of Chicago. It is a city of approximately 200,000, and as such, is confronted with some of the same crimes that police officers deal within urban areas throughout the country. Commander Ziman recognizes the predicament and gravity of what law enforcement organizations face, particularly as it relates to the public's fading trust. She understands the significance of law enforcement agencies doing all they can to regularly demonstrate their adherence to prescribed police protocols, as well as the importance of police officers demonstrating allegiance to their sworn oath through their personal actions. It is after all the preservation of trust that affects the officer's reputation in the communities where he or she is assigned.

Commander Ziman's observations are widely shared not only by members of the law enforcement community, but also by a majority of the American people, who are acutely aware of the rising incidents of police corruption, brutality, and scandal. Concern continues to grow as citizens ponder whether the law enforcement hierarchy has the capacity to restrain a situation that appears to some as fast becoming out of control and potentially spreading to the highest ranks of the criminal justice system. Here is what Commander Ziman had to say about police officers, and the significance of the bond that is essential if they are to effectively serve and protect the communities that they serve.

> The ramifications of trust being eroded in our community are devastating. Citizens rely on the police (an arm of the government) to practice legitimate authority in applications of law. Citizens trade some freedoms for this protection (i.e. 4th Amendment Laws of Arrest, Search and Seizure) because they trust that the police are working within the parameters of the law and in their best interest. Citizens give the police the power to uphold the laws outlined in the constitution in exchange for protection and enforcement.
>
> When the government exceeds the boundaries and abuses power, the citizen's extreme reaction is to overthrow the government. The response to the Rodney King beating in 1992 is a good example

of this. The public starting rioting in the streets as a result of the actions of the L.A. police officers.

When the police undermine legitimacy, the public responds in protest. When this happens, civil unrest is a consequence.

When the police act honorably and with service, justice and fundamental fairness as their guide, the trust strengthens. Even when discharging the unpleasant but necessary duties of the office such as search and arrest, citizens accept those actions if they are done with equity and adherence to laws.

People respect power when power is derived from justice. Historian and moralist Lord Acton expressed this opinion:

"Power tends to corrupt, and absolute power corrupts absolutely."

When all power is given to one entity, the theory is that man inevitably falls prey to corruption. This is why power cannot be absolute. We must have checks and balances within the hierarchy to protect us from dictatorship.

When police officers enter this profession because they are power-driven, that power becomes absolutely corrupt. Not only do police officers have the power to take away a person's freedom (incarceration), they can take a human life as long as it fits within the parameters of the law. If you think of the awesome responsibility that befalls those acts, you want it only in the hands of those who are worthy.

Because our officers on the front line see the worst of humanity, one can begin to understand how seeing the corrosion can skew an officer and ultimately test their will. At times when the criminal justice system fails, a police officer may feel they have to compromise the constitution and the laws to ensure justice. But the ends do not justify the means so police officers need to be reminded of their purpose and their mission so they continue to fight for justice justly.

Gone are the days of the "thin blue line" where police officers are blindly loyal to one another. Instead, the "thin blue line" is morphing into a positive and honorable litmus test where the police guard themselves by policing one another. We stand together in virtue and honor but we part with the officer who goes wrong. Our "thin blue line" should comprise only those who make the badge shine brighter—not those who tarnish it.[7]

If Commander Ziman's statement moves you to wonder where we are now—that is, as it relates to the public's cynicism for police officers—it's not so surprising. This is especially true given existing and proposed legislation that tends to attribute blame to urban America, and particularly to minorities, for many of the societal ills that affect contemporary society. For example, as pointed out in a column that I wrote for *The Voice*, a local hometown newspaper that gives fair and equal space to opinions that are sometimes contrary to that of other print media, there is a tendency to both blame and target minorities and the economically disadvantaged for prosecutorial efforts related to the sale and distribution of illicit drugs.

In 2014, Illinois House Republicans proposed legislation that would use the ill-gotten gains derived from the sale of illicit drugs to fund substance abuse treatment programs. In doing so, they would help those addicted to heroin, methamphetamines, and other deadly drugs. Efforts so far to eradicate the highly addictive drugs center on the belief that Chicago gangs and people from underprivileged Chicago West Side neighborhoods are the sole suppliers of illicit drugs that make their way to suburban communities.

While there is irrefutable evidence that the infamous "heroin highway" is a major pipeline for illicit drugs that contribute to heroin addiction in suburban communities, studies conducted by the U.S. Department of Health and Human Services (HHS), Substance Abuse and Mental Health Services Administration, counter the premise. For example, HHS studies reveal that people of every color and ethnicity are involved in selling illegal drugs, including heroin. Nonetheless, the War on Drugs fails to consider that well-heeled and established suburban drug networks sell, manufacture, and distribute illegal drugs, including addictive prescription drugs.

Equally important is the effort to prove to the public that the thousands of blacks and browns incarcerated in America's expanding prison-industrial complex represents solid proof that the criminal justice system has identified the source of illegal drug distribution. The reality is that many minorities that currently fill U.S. prisons to capacity are themselves addicts jailed for possessing small amounts of illegal drugs. America's War on Drugs not only branded people of color as the chief suppliers of heroin and methamphetamines, but it also deliberately adopted the strategy in order to reduce anxiety among the general public. Decades later, the tactic is backfiring, and is increasingly seen as a disservice to the American people.

As it turns out, the incarceration of minority drug offenders has not only created a rapidly growing financial opportunity for savvy investors, but also a legal method of controlling downtrodden minorities. According to Michelle Alexander, author of *The New Jim Crow: Mass Incarceration in the Age of Color Blindness*, as it relates to black men, just as their ancestors were during the Jim Crow era, blacks are relegated to a lifetime of second-class citizenship. Due to encounters with the criminal justice system, they are not considered for employment opportunities, are denied access to housing, education, and public benefits, and in many cases are deemed ineligible to vote. Alexander, who has clerked for Justice Harry A. Blackmun on the U.S. Supreme Court and for Chief Judge Abner Mikva on the D.C. Circuit of the U.S. Court of Appeals, believes that there is a new racial caste system in America that replaces the old Jim Crow. The New York best-selling author persuasively asserts, "I came to see that mass incarceration in the United States had, in fact, emerged as a stunningly comprehensive and well-disguised system of racialized social control that functions in a manner strikingly similar to Jim Crow."[8]

Disenfranchisement has long been directly connected with second-class citizenship. Moreover, connecting drug distribution to race and supporting the demonization of people of color constitutes an extremely effective scheme to control entire populations. I believe that Alexander's broad examination of the American penal system, one that imprisons over two million people including hundreds of thousands of black males and females, should serve as a wake-up call.

While minorities were fast becoming the face of illicit drug distribution, a gang of Hollywood scriptwriters were busy developing the hit television series *Breaking Bad*. In it, Walter White, a fictionalized white suburban manufacturer and peddler of crystal methamphetamine, was infused with a sense of honor, integrity, and moral righteousness. The actions of White, who makes and deals crystal meth because he has terminal lung cancer, are marketed as somehow different and acceptable. White's criminal deeds are cleverly couched and differentiated from inner-city drug dealers of color. White is looking out for his family, making sure that after he succumbs to the ravages of an incurable cancer, money will not be among their worries. Ironically, White's dramatized predicament is a reality, and a life-and-death struggle of some inner-city drug dealers. Frankly, the one discernable difference is that minority drug dealers have come to symbolize a financial boon for the prison-industrial complex.

Now juxtapose the fictional portrayal of White to that of a four-year-old Chicago boy who was used to illustrate out-of-control gangbanging and gun violence. In Chicago, news coverage of weekend shooting deaths and casualties can sometimes resemble a war correspondent's report from a hot battle zone. It is also a city where death and mayhem take on an entertainment quality. In one such case several years ago, CBS affiliate WBBM aired a video clip that prominently featured the interview of a four-year-old black boy in the immediate wake of the shooting death of a 16-year-old boy in the child's gang-ridden Chicago community. With a microphone shoved in his face by a freelance photographer, the boy was asked, "What are you going to do when you get older?" To which the boy is shown to respond, "I'm going to have me a gun!"

The video went viral, and many Chicagoans were shocked, believing that they were observing an individual destined for a life of gangbanging and street violence. However, it was later revealed that the boy's comments had been edited, and that the entirety of his response would have depicted the child in an entirely different way. Here's what the four-year old boy actually said in response to the question:

Reporter: "Boy, you ain't scared of nothing! Damn! When you get older are you going to stay away from all these guns?"

Boy: "No."

Reporter: "No? What are you going to do when you get older?"

Boy: "I'm going to have me a gun!"

Reporter: "You are! Why do you want to do that?"

Boy: "I'm going to be the police!"[9]

After it was revealed that the video had been edited to, in all probability, sensationalize the story, the news outlet apologized for its airing.

Princeton University professor Cornel West may have said it best when describing what we are up against: "There is no doubt that if young white people were incarcerated at the same rates as young black people, the issue would be a national emergency. But it is also true that if young black middle- and upper-class people were incarcerated at the same rates as young black poor people, black leaders would focus much more on the prison-industrial complex."[10]

I firmly believe that efforts to eradicate illegal drugs that fail to take into account the flourishing suburban drug market, where OxyContin, heroin, and methamphetamines are sold from gated communities, will miss the mark.[11] It brings us back to the trust factor and what has caused the soaring suspicion, particularly among people of color, toward the criminal justice system, from the police officer responding to calls for assistance, to the magistrate that decides what, if any, sentence to impose on the accused.

In the chapters that follow, a highly regarded, longtime employee of the criminal courts offers an insightful assessment into the day-to-day operation of the criminal courts division. Because of the individual's sensitive position, that person asked to maintain anonymity.

Relying on my years of experience, I firmly believe that most young men and women who are currently in the system are intentionally portrayed as devoid of conscience. Yet, I contend that the overwhelming majority know right from wrong, but make a conscious decision against doing what is right. Having said that, there are factual accounts of wayward police officers who terrorize citizens and engage in criminal acts. What's more is that ample evidence indicates that corruption within police departments throughout the United States is systemic and extraordinarily difficult to stamp out. The disproportionate number of arrests in conjunction with circumstances, when linked with racism and misuse of police power, are horrific and difficult for the person caught in the middle to overcome. Reducing recidivism and changing the mindset of law enforcement will require radical change from within, beginning with the officer on the street.[12]

From the eye-opening insider point of view to what the general public knows about police corruption, it is appropriate to conclude that law enforcement agencies face a daunting challenge. For instance, in some Chicago communities, lawlessness and the disregard for police officers are so extreme that in 2013, after a night when 13 innocent people, including a three-year-old boy, were shot with an assault rifle, Chicago's police superintendent finally opened to the idea of supplementing the city's 8,000-strong police department with National Guard troops. What many perceived as a shocking about-face and confirmation that the CPD is incapable of containing violence, in some areas of the city, only scratches the surface. However, when one looks beyond the violence, and instead lends focus to its source, the public's lack of respect for both police officers and the entire criminal justice system is among the top contributing factors.

NOTES

1. The Black Commentator, http://www.blackcommentator.com/67/67_hampton_pf.html (accessed January 28, 2014).

2. William Lee, "Chicago Cop Struck Fear in South Side from 1934–51," *Chicago Tribune*, July 21, 2013, http://articles.chicagotribune.com/2013-07-21/news/ct-met-two-gun-pete-20130721_1_chicago-cop-south-side-wabash-avenue (accessed January 12, 2014).

3. Quincy Jones, *Q: The Autobiography of Quincy Jones* (New York: Doubleday, 2001).

4. Dan Wetzel, "Eagles Need to Say if DeSean Jackson's Release Was Tied to 'Gang' Report," Yahoo Sports, http://sports.yahoo.com/news/eagles-need-to-address-perception-that-desean-jackson-s-release-is-related-to-report-about-gang-ties-192128226.html?vp=1 (accessed April 2, 2014).

5. Kent Babb, "Redskins Wide Receiver DeSean Jackson's Path to the NFL Wound through Gang Territory," *Washington Post*, April 16, 2014.

6. Sarah Moughty, "17 Justice Dept. Investigations into Police Departments Worldwide," PBS, *Frontline*, http://www.pbs.org/wgbh/pages/frontline/criminal-justice/law-disorder/17-justice-dept-investigations-into-police-departments-nationwide/ (accessed January 28, 2014).

7. Narrative by Kristen Ziman, Aurora Police commander, March 31, 2014.

8. Michelle Alexander, *The New Jim Crow: Mass Incarceration in the Age of Colorblindness* (New York: New Press, 2014).

9. Bob Butler, July 19, 2011, Maynard Institute, http://mije.org/health/young-guns (accessed October 26, 2014).

10. Ibid.

11. Anthony Stanford, "Flourishing Suburban Drug Market Part of the Problem," *The Voice*, April 3, 2014.

12. Anonymous interview, April 23, 2014.

2

•❖•

The History of Police Corruption

"Gentlemen, get the thing straight for once and for all.
The policeman isn't there to create disorder; the policeman is
there to preserve disorder."[1]

POLICE CORRUPTION VERSUS POLICE CRIMES

It is important to first understand and then to distinguish between police
misconduct and criminal acts committed by police officers. Though the
line is sometimes blurred, police corruption is generally considered to be
an act in which a law enforcement officer participates in activities that
benefit them personally, and most often financially. Examples of police
corruption include the acceptance of bribes for ignoring crimes, such as
drug dealing, prostitution, and gambling. Other examples of police corruption are the selective pursuit of criminal investigations and the falsification
of police reports to influence the direction of an ongoing criminal investigation. Again, this is typically done for personal financial gain, or other
incentives such as promotion. One way that police corruption differs from
the crimes committed by individuals in the general population occurs
when police officers are involved in criminal acts such as murder, rape,
domestic violence, and theft. When law enforcement officials commit
crimes of this nature, it damages the public trust as well as law enforcement
morale.

I recall a bizarre incident that occurred as I was driving home from work on a Chicago expressway in the early 1970s. It just happened to have been a payday, and before leaving work, I had placed a U.S. savings bond in my shirt pocket. Just minutes from home, in my rearview mirror, I saw the flashing lights of a police car and then heard the siren. I pulled over and waited for the officer to approach. The officer said that I'd been speeding and asked to see my driver's license. When complying with the officer's request, all of sudden things got weird when he accused me of trying to bribe him.

Entirely baffled, I asked what had given him that idea, and assured him that this was not the case. I racked my brain in an attempt to figure out what he was referring to. However, before I could formulate a way to diffuse what had become a precarious situation, he pointed to the savings bond protruding from my shirt pocket. I explained that I'd been paid earlier that day and had received the monthly savings bond along with my check. He listened, and when I was done explaining, thinking that surely the matter had been resolved, I was stunned when the officer said, "Okay, slip me 10 bucks, and don't speed again." When I politely refused, he issued a warning for speeding.

It is not so much that people are naïve, but many grow up being told to respect police officers and to believe in the criminal justice system. Yet, it is remarkable how a single incident can change a person's viewpoint and forever alter their perception of the police and, in some cases, the entire criminal justice system. To deduce that the epidemic of police corruption, especially in urban areas, is having an adverse impact on individuals and entire communities by affecting the relationship that police and law enforcement organizations have with the public is not far-fetched. For instance, in the black community, cooperation with the police, as it relates to reporting crime or identifying those who commit criminal acts, is largely viewed as a betrayal of allegiance to the race and those terrorized by "The Man." While it sounds absurd, to some extreme, many people view the police as enemies of the people, and they are in some cases justified in their perception.

There are innumerable accounts of police officers across the country who willfully engage in criminal activity. One standout is former Chicago police officer William Hanhardt, who to this day remains the highest-ranking Chicago police officer convicted of criminal wrongdoing. In 2002, Hanhardt was sentenced to 12 years in prison for running a jewelry-theft ring that, over the course of 20 years, stole millions of dollars in prized gems. No small-time player, Hanhardt was referred to as the Outfit's Top Cop, because as a highly decorated chief of Chicago Police

Department detectives, he testified as a defense witness in the trial of Chicago mob killers Tony and Michael Spilotro. Sometime after a mistrial of the brothers was declared and they were subsequently released from prison, the brothers were killed.[2]

In another spectacular case involving a police officer, disgraced former narcotics officer Glenn Lewellen was found guilty by a federal jury of drug conspiracy charges, and of participating in a drug-trafficking operation. Calling it "Another Black Eye for Chicago Police," Courthouse News Service reported that, "According to the 2010 criminal indictment, defendant Officer Lewellen held himself out as a police officer when obtaining wholesale quantities of cocaine in the Chicago area. He has been charged with racketeering conspiracy, conspiracy to distribute cocaine, kidnapping, robbery of 100 kilograms of cocaine and cash, and obstruction of justice for concealing the activities of the drug operation."[3]

The criminal acts committed by Lewellen and Hanhardt barely scratch the surface of police officers that misuse the power and trust bestowed to them in order to perpetrate criminal acts for personal gain. Lewellen and Hanhardt exemplify the type of police corruption that goes directly to the struggle, being waged by law enforcement organizations throughout the United States, to find ways to preclude such individuals from, in the first place, taking an oath to serve and protect.

Flaunting law enforcement authority with the willful intent of taking advantage of others comes under the heading of police misconduct. In this instance, it is generally seen in cases of police brutality, excessive force, and is generally perceived as a crime against society. When former Chicago police commander Jon Burge was convicted and sentenced to more than four years in federal prison for covering up the torture and abuse of criminal suspects, Burge's action had and continues to have an enormous negative effect on the morale and reputation of Chicago Police Department (CPD) personnel. Sadly, it took more than three decades for an elected Chicago official to formally apologize for the horrendous misdeeds perpetrated on Burge's watch. Mayor Rahm Emanuel did so following approval of a multimillion-dollar settlement to two men that decades earlier had given false confessions to a murder after being tortured by police under Burge's command. In September 2013 in a candid statement, and several years into his first term as Chicago's mayor, Emanuel referred to Burge's reign of terror as a "dark chapter."[4]

A University of Illinois report disclosed the cost to local taxpayers for defending the city of Chicago against charges of police misconduct lawsuits and out-of court settlements related to the Burge deluge of litigation, pointing out that, "Over the last decade, police misconduct lawsuits against the city and out-of-court settlements have cost taxpayers several hundreds of millions of dollars at a time when all levels of government have to cut services and raise taxes." According to the alarming report, defending cops against litigation has cost Chicago taxpayers in excess of $82.5 million since 2003, and "Jon Burge cases have cost local taxpayers more than $53 million since 1998."[5] However, according to the report, Chicagoans are not the only ones paying for the bad behavior of police officers. New York, Oakland, Los Angeles, Milwaukee, Cleveland, and Denver are also mentioned.

To illustrate the effect of payouts to settle claims made against police, the New York City comptroller reported that for fiscal year 2011 alone, the city paid $185.6 million in claims, with the number of claims rising as a result of the city's controversial stop-and-frisk program. According to the report, in connection with the handling by police of Occupy demonstrations, the city of Oakland paid settlements estimated at $13,149,000. The story is much the same in Los Angeles, where police brutality cases like that of Rodney King in 1991 continue to make national news with payouts to civilians well into the millions of dollars. Having said that, it is not only the public's demand to bring to an end the misconduct and brutality suffered by citizens at the hands of some police officers that behave badly, but also the burden that has put at risk the financial integrity of some municipalities.

Moreover, keeping cops honest and battling against the sinister perception, suspicion, and cynicism produced by events like the Burge-era crimes, particularly as it relates to minorities, linger in the minds of civilians. There is no doubt that the damage to the relationship between minorities and law enforcement in Chicago is directly related to Burge's rule over minority criminal suspects and a shattering of the guarantee of civil liberties to all citizens. By 2013, Burge's offenses had saddled Chicago taxpayers with a huge financial burden, leaving them to pay settlements, estimated at $85 million, associated with making whole the wrongly convicted. The Cook County government alone has paid an estimated $11 million related to torture cases in which they were named as plaintiffs. Ironically, the excessive taxpayer expenditures do not include the millions of dollars spent to defend Burge against the lawsuits.

Aside from the monetary loss of taxpayer dollars, and most disconcerting to the public, is Burge's repeated misuse of police powers in ordering or perpetrating, for well over two decades, the torture of more than 100 criminal suspects. According to the *Chicago Reader*, Burge, along with 64 other police officers, used "electric shock, suffocation, burnings, attacks on the genitals, severe beating, and mock executions" to compel confessions from criminal suspects. One Chicago detective put it this way: "It was a reign of terror. I don't know what Kristallnacht was like, but this was probably close." A detective who knew a number of the officers accused of being members of Burge's crew said this about men that were fellow police officers: "They're a lot of brawn, not much brains. I went to school with them, I like them, but they're not too smart. Their idea is you go out and pick up 2,000 pounds of nigger and eventually you'll get the right one."[6]

As indicated, the CPD is not alone; there are many reports, opinions, and research studies related to the occurrence and severity of police wrong-doing and incidents of criminality by law enforcement personnel. In fact, according to one report by News One for Black America ranking the most corrupt U.S. police officers, Jon Burge comes in at number two, with the infamous number-one ranking going to former New Orleans police officers. In 2011, the report named the following individuals among the most corrupt police officers in America:

1. Robert Gisevius, Kenneth Bowen, and Anthony Villavaso, former New Orleans police officers charged with killing a 17-year-old during Hurricane Katrina. They were found guilty of lying and false prosecution in a conspiracy to cover up the killing of James Brissette, and sentenced to between 38 and 65 years in prison.
2. Jon Burge, who supervised the torture of hundreds of black men between 1972 and 1991 resulting in false confessions, increased distrust of law enforcement, and a tremendous financial cost to the city of Chicago.
3. Former Los Angeles Police Department (LAPD) Rampart division police officers David Mack and Rafael Perez, who also belonged to the Bloods street gang. Mack was the recipient of the LAPD's Medal of Honor for killing a drug dealer who allegedly pulled a gun on him. However, he was convicted of bank robbery and believed to be involved in the murder of rapper Notorious BIG. Perez was convicted of framing an unarmed gang member and stealing a large quantity of cocaine from a LAPD evidence locker.
4. Former Chicago Police officer Joseph Miedzianowski, who served as a drug kingpin and used law enforcement information to shake down drug dealers. The rogue cop was convicted of drug conspiracy and racketeering, and sentenced to life in prison. According to the *Chicago Tribune*, when pronouncing sentence on Miedzianowski, U.S. district judge Blanche Manning said, "There comes a time in every person's life to embrace what he or she has become, to check

the compass of his heart, to remember paths traveled . . . I'm afraid to discover, Mr. Miedzianowski, what you are now, sir. You used your powers to infect a trusting society."[7]

5. New York City police officers Louis Eppolito and Stephen Caracappa, who worked for the Mafia. Caracappa was assigned to the Organized Crime Homicide Unit and was responsible for investigating the people whom he worked for. Both were hit men working inside the NYPD for the Lucchese crime family. Eppolito and Caracappa were convicted of obstruction of justice, extortion, racketeering, and eight counts of murder and conspiracy.[8]

In the chapters that follow, examples of egregious police misconduct, corruption, and an assortment of criminality are described, in detail, in order to validate the reality and pervasiveness of what plagues our criminal justice system and erodes the public's trust in the police and law enforcement organizations.

POLICE CORRUPTION IN AMERICA

Whether police corruption in America is an unavoidable consequence connected to the price that society must pay to maintain an orderly society is subject to rigorous debate. However, it is an enormously important question when considering whether police corruption is merely a reflection of the crime that is committed in the civilian population, or uniquely associated with the law enforcement culture, and a by-product of the authority conferred on police officers and the entire criminal justice system.

Considering that the onset of police corruption began during the mid-1800s, almost immediately after the first police departments were formed in America, there is no sign that the debate or problem will soon end. It is also worth mentioning that during the infancy of America's law enforcement formation, political parties controlled municipal governments as well as an assortment of organizations that directly interfaced with the public. Equally ironic is that the creation of police departments was initially necessitated by the criminal behavior of political powerhouses such as New York City's Tammany Hall. That said, there came a time in America when political corruption and graft, like that which prevailed under the infamous Tammany Hall leader William M. Tweed, would infiltrate police departments and eventually increase the public's wariness toward police officers, and law enforcement organizations overall.

According to the official website of the city of Boston, the Boston Police Department (BPD), is the nation's oldest police department.

It began in 1838, and was modeled on the London Police force developed by Sir Robert Peele. The BPD was originally responsible for "the care of the streets, the care of the common sewers, and the care of the vaults, and whatever else affects the health, security, and comfort of the city."[9] The chief of the original BPD had 260 police officers under his command. BPD officers while on duty were armed with a blue-and-white, six-foot pole for their protection and a "police rattle" to sound the call for assistance.

As police corruption became more prevalent, it became routine for some police officers to look the other way for personal financial gain, and to allow social vices like prostitution and gambling to become the norm, and something tolerated by the general population. In municipalities across America, dishonesty within police departments was commonplace and accepted to a great extent by the people. Dishonest police officers who sometimes worked as independent operatives provided protection for individuals who were involved in illicit activities. Crooked police officers who demanded money from the individuals perpetrating crimes became part of the problem, an early indication of how widespread police corruption would ultimately become. The flourishing multifaceted, felonious undertakings of the underworld, and the laissez-faire attitude of law enforcement agencies at the highest level to reel in crime, would eventually necessitate drastic measures. In order to quell public demand and to counter the growing problem of police corruption, the formation of in-house policing efforts like internal affairs divisions, also known as "rat squads," became common and received voter support.

From the very start, it appears that police corruption was generally viewed as part and parcel of the law enforcement culture and eventually considered as the cost of doing business. In fact, one gets the impression that corruption existed in all police departments. However, there were also those who, early on, vehemently opposed the pervasive nature of police corruption, viewing it as ruinous immoral behavior that affected the integrity of law enforcement. Regrettably, those who believed the activities of police officers to be harmless and somewhat exaggerated by a small percentage of people muffled the voices of the outspoken minority. Consequently, as criminal activity in the general population grew, it was only a matter of time before the criminal element infiltrated the hierarchy of police departments, and that reports of criminal activity among rank-and-file police officers were more widespread, and their misdeeds increasingly daring.

Eventually, the overall mindset of the public began to change as frustration with the status quo turned toward the politicians who controlled law enforcement agencies. In a twist of irony, fueled by the public's demand to reform law enforcement, powerful politicians became a catalyst for such reform. The public cried out for an end to the unethical practices of police officers and law enforcement officials, and that something be done to combat the unlawful activities that were enticing police officers to participate in those pursuits. The public's demand helped to create the momentum and political will needed to establish police commissions, civil service exams, and other reforms focused on the procedure needed to clean up law enforcement organizations.

Methods aimed at weeding out inferior personality types and more effectively blocking the entry of undesirables into the law enforcement ranks would evolve over time. Incrementally instituted enhancements throughout law enforcement were seen as a symbolic step, and one that the public believed had come about as a result of their demand for change. The effort to better screen police officers was deemed by many as the first and the essential measure needed to gain control of law enforcement agencies that were plagued by corrupt cops.

Unfortunately, when the Eighteenth Amendment was ratified and the National Prohibition Act of 1919 (more commonly referred to as the Volstead Act) became the law of the land, it ushered in a period of lawlessness and widespread corruption throughout the criminal justice system. The Eighteenth Amendment succinctly stated that "the manufacture, sale, or transportation of intoxicating liquors within, the importation thereof into, or the exportation thereof from the United States and all territory subject to the jurisdiction thereof for beverage purposes is hereby prohibited" and that "Congress and the several States shall have concurrent power to enforce this article by appropriate legislation."[10] Ironically, the Eighteenth Amendment spawned a cottage industry of criminal activity that would eventually penetrate law enforcement agencies throughout the United States, as well as the creation of various societal problems. Moreover, the practically unhindered authority of police officers at the time of the amendment created the potential, and eventuality, of a wave of widespread police corruption directly related to Prohibition. There were individuals that had forecasted the inevitable evils of Prohibition. However, it took others time to realize that neither the law enforcement community nor the American people had understood the potential repercussions that would eventually come as a result of the Eighteenth Amendment.

The Volstead Act created the prospect for a huge monetary gain derived from unlawful endeavors associated with the illegal manufacturing and distribution of alcohol. The nefarious participants were bootleggers, corrupt politicians, police officers, and an indulging public, all who adversely affected efforts to enforce the law. The relationships that were started as a result of the Volstead Act between police officers and the criminal element were disastrous, and in the end, they weakened the authority of law enforcement and the public's respect for the criminal justice system. The taint created by the Volstead Act, and damage that it caused required extraordinary efforts to reverse it, including a campaign to root out police and political corruption.

Almost a century before Frank Serpico, the celebrated and despised New York City police officer who singlehandedly cracked the blue wall of silence maintained by police officers who lied about or turned a blind eye to criminal acts committed by police officers, there was Chicago attorney Frank Loesch. Legendary in the annals of Chicago's storied crime-fighting history, Loesch lead an unprecedented and epic attempt to combat organized crime, political corruption, and police wrongdoing.

Loesch began his illustrious crime-fighting career in the early 1890s, when he acted on behalf of the Pennsylvania Railroad Company in Chicago. Early on, Loesch had recognized the potential for graft and corruption by politicians and publicly decried attempts by some members of the Chicago City Council to extort money from the railroad. For the rest of his career, Loesch fearlessly fought corruption in Chicago's courthouses and police stations. In a December 2011 *Chicago Tribune* article, columnist Stephan Benzkofer wrote about Loesch, "The system was rigged against him—corrupt cops, public officials and judges stymied his investigations. As acquittals piled up, his opponents argued he was on politically motivated hunting expeditions. But he never quit."[11]

According to Benzkofer, during the infamous days of Al Capone's gangland Chicago, Loesch served as a special prosecutor and was elected president of the Chicago Crime Commission that he had helped found in 1919. However, Loesch's success against Capone's widening corruption, and alliances with corrupt politicians such as Chicago mayor "Big Bill" Thompson, would not come until the 1930s, when Capone was placed at the top of the Chicago Crime Commission's list of public enemies. The Chicago Crime Commission's designation of 28 men brought pressure on the police commissioner and law enforcement officials to finally deal with those labeled as "public enemies" and as a threat to the general public.

In 1931, when taking on the Eighteenth Amendment and arguing that it was unattainable in its present form, Loesch forcefully asserted his belief related to corruption, and the impact that it was having on law enforcement:

A strong reason, among others, why I favor immediate steps being taken to revise the Amendment is in order to destroy the power of the murderous, criminal organizations flourishing all over the country upon the enormous profits made in bootleg liquor traffic. Those profits are the main source of the corruption funds that cement the alliance between crime and politics and corrupt the law enforcing agencies in every populous city.

Those criminal octopus organizations have now grown so audacious owing to their long immunity from prosecutions for their crimes that they seek to make bargains with law enforcing officers and even with judges of our courts to be allowed for a price to continue their criminal activities unmolested by the law.

Those organizations of murderers and arch criminals can only be destroyed when their bootleg liquor profits are taken from them. So long as the Eighteenth Amendment remains in its present rigid form the nation, the states, the municipalities, the individual citizen, are helpless to get out of reach of their poisonous breaths and slimy tentacles.

If not soon crushed those criminal organizations may become as they are now seeking to become super-governments and so beyond the reach of the ordinary processes of the law.[12]

The "criminal octopus organizations" that Loesch referred to involved local and state agencies that had been polluted by the steady flow of cash derived from bootlegging enterprises operating throughout the city. Loesch and other law enforcement officials who were not corrupted by the unlawful businesses linked to Prohibition were for a time up against not only the individuals who were running the illegal operations, but also those who had been sworn to uphold law and order, respect civil liberties, and root out illegal activities. It was indeed a challenge for Loesch and other law-abiding law enforcement professionals, who were trying to uphold law and order and to prevent further incursion of lawlessness into America's law enforcement community.

In the end, the common sense of the American people prevailed, and Prohibition was deemed unenforceable. When this occurred, the previously ballyhooed Eighteenth Amendment, once touted as a necessary reform to save America, was repealed and came to be seen as a monumental failure, and major contributor to political, public and police corruption. However, by the time it was agreed that the amendment was having an adverse effect on the general population, including contributing to public lawlessness, police criminality, and moral degeneration, much of the damage had already been done. Unfortunately, the 1933 repeal came too late, and a once naïve and trusting public, as it relates to wholesomeness of law enforcement, was rife with skepticism and distrust in the political system, law enforcement, and, in some instances, the total criminal justice system.

Some 40 years after the demise of the Eighteenth Amendment, and at a time when the public's trust in law enforcement agencies had to an extent sobered from the effects of prohibition and Al Capone's lawlessness, along comes New York City police officer Frank Serpico. In 1971, the whistle-blowing police officer gained celebrity status by bringing attention to the New York City Police Department (NYPD) when he complained about pervasive corruption from within. Serpico's allegation that NYPD officers were, on a large scale, involved in drug-related crimes, drug trafficking, illegal searches and other criminal behavior set in motion New York City mayor John V. Lindsay's formation of the Knapp Commission to investigate NYPD police corruption. Serpico's relentless criticism and compelling testimony under oath eventually led to a finding by the Knapp Commission that widespread corruption indeed existed within the NYPD. The Knapp Commission findings were believed by many to be indicative of systemic corruption in police departments throughout America. Years later, Serpico would say that, "The fight for justice against corruption is never easy. It never has been and never will be. It exacts a toll on our self, our families, our friends, and especially our children. In the end, I believe, as in my case, the price we pay is well worth holding on to our dignity."[13]

By the time Serpico was done, the idealization of "Officer Friendly" had been obliterated, helped along by sensational news stories related to police corruption across the country. American naiveté was replaced by the harsh reality that every stripe of criminal act imaginable, including murder, rape, spousal abuse, theft, drug dealing, arson and more, has been alleged against and, in many cases, proven to have been committed by the police officers who vowed to serve and protect the public.

Though it is hard to believe that reputation of police officers could get any worse, it did in 2013, when New York City police officer Gilberto Valle broke new ground for degenerate criminal acts committed by a police officer—or, for that matter, the human species. Valle was accused and found guilty of charges that he plotted to kidnap, cook, and eat women, including his own wife. Commenting on Valle's depraved indifference, details of the gruesome case, and the 2013 guilty verdict, U.S. attorney Preet Bharara said that, "Today, a unanimous jury found that Gilberto Valle's detailed and specific plans to abduct women for the purpose of committing grotesque crimes were very real, and that he was guilty as charged. The Internet is a forum for the free exchange of ideas, but it does not confer immunity for plotting crimes and taking steps to carry out those crimes."[14]

Though contemplated, but discovered before he was able to carry out the monstrous crime, Valle's criminality ranks highest among the most heinous crimes committed by a police officer. Valle is in the company of another police officer whose crime, trial, and conviction played out in the tabloids for many months. Now a convicted murderer, former Bolingbrook, Illinois, police sergeant Drew Peterson, a publicity-seeking sociopath, was sentenced in 2013 for murdering his third ex-wife, Kathleen Savio. As of this writing, he was also implicated in the disappearance of his fourth wife, Stacy Peterson.

In laying out his case for the maximum allowable sentence, Will County state's attorney James Glasgow told Judge Edward Burmila this about Peterson: "Obviously he violated that oath at the highest level. He betrayed the public trust, the sacred trust. And that, judge, is what I think you can place the highest weight on when you contemplate an appropriate sentence in this case."[15] Indicating that he had considered Peterson's 30 years as a police officer and military service, Judge Burmila sentenced Peterson to 38 years in prison. It is difficult to fathom a worse demonstration of wanton criminal behavior by someone sworn to uphold law and order, yet there are many more.

For instance, in 2013, a shocked nation watched as a former disgruntled Los Angeles police officer, Christopher Dorner, went on a deadly shooting rampage, wounding three police officers, killing one officer and the daughter of a Los Angeles police captain, and her fiancé. The nation was riveted by the national media coverage of the rapidly unfolding events related to the effort to take Dorner into custody. Early reports indicated that Dorner had been fired by the Los Angeles Police Department in 2009, when the LAPD Board of Rights concluded that he had filed a false complaint against a fellow officer, saying that she had kicked a suspect in custody.

Dorner's revengeful and murderous tear through the California hills, and at times his bizarre manifesto that accused the LAPD of widespread corruption, racism, and hiding acts of excessive force and police brutality as well as other criminal acts from the public, became an integral part of one of the largest manhunts in the history of California law enforcement. The former LAPD officer, who vowed to keep killing police until his name was cleared, committed crimes that are on a number of levels very disturbing. Los Angeles law enforcement professionals reopened an investigation into the charges leading to Dorner's dismissal and taking Dorner's accusations seriously. First, and aside from the brutality with which he killed three innocent people, some of Dorner's claims are exceedingly troubling, because to some onlookers, they not only have a ring of truth, but they also are reminiscent of the LAPD's troubled history of police corruption.

Dorner's desperate and sometimes rambling manifesto does more than to merely pierce the blue wall. In it Dorner tries to knock the wall down by asserting the existence of systemic corruption inside the LAPD. Dorner's contention echoes a concern held by political rivals, and one that is not easily dismissed within Los Angeles's minority community. As a result, LAPD's hierarchy was forced to respond by reopening the investigation into Dorner's firing, and in doing so, stressed complete transparency. LAPD chief Charlie Beck issued a statement: "I am aware of the ghosts of the LAPD's past and one of my biggest concerns is that they will be resurrected by Dorner's allegations of racism within the department . . . Therefore, I feel we need to also publicly address Dorner's allegations regarding his termination of employment."[16]

Crimes like those of Dorner, Peterson, and Valle do more than to breach the canon of law enforcement ethics. Their crimes and those committed by other police officers expose a cold reality about police officers that many would prefer not to deal with. However, it reminds us that, like the general population, inside the law enforcement community, there are individuals who are capable of perpetrating any manner of crime against humanity. Yet, the clear difference is that when criminal acts are done by police officers, the aftereffect can be tremendously damaging to society as a whole, eroding the public's sense of trust and wellbeing.

For example, when a police officer commits an act of domestic violence, besides its serious effect on the victim, extended family, and community, for reasons that are not entirely understood, it lessens the severity of domestic abuse in the eyes of the general population. According to noted author, advocate, and feminist Diane Wetendorg, when a police officer commits an act of domestic violence, it is secreted and treated as a private matter within the police family. According to Wetendorg:

> Many of the qualities valued in on-duty police officers can make them dangerous domestic violence offenders. All abusers employ similar methods to control and abuse their intimate partners. Officers however, have skills and tactics not commonly possessed by civilians. Professional training in force, weapons, intimidation, interrogation and surveillance—along with the cultural climate—become a

dangerous and potentially lethal combination in a domestic situation. Victims face the bias of law enforcement agencies and the legal system, psychological intimidation, and a high lethality risk.[17]

Considered to be most troubling are the violent crimes committed by police, such as murder, assault, and physical and sexual abuse. Each time a police officer is accused or found guilty of committing a heinous crime, the underpinnings of America's law enforcement foundation are threatened. Moreover, when police officers commit especially evil criminal acts, like the atrocities planned by Valle and committed by Peterson and Dorner, our collective societal psyche is jarred, and consequently we are overcome by an unsettling sense of unspoken insecurity.

Aside from the damage that police corruption does to the morale of honest rank-and-file police officers, including tarnishing the reputation of hardworking men and women in uniform, it also legitimizes crime for a segment of society. The harm that bad cops do and the illegal acts that they commit have an incalculable negative and lasting effect on the impressionable minds of our children. Bit by bit, over the long haul, it can cause them to suffer the adverse effects caused by confusion and distort their view of social order over time, in some instances diminishing their sense of morality.

Criminal involvement by police officers of any kind is distressing, but there is also something about corrupt police officers that, from the perspective of the average citizen, is unnerving. To the human mind, it can be extraordinarily difficult, after being conditioned to recognize law enforcement officials as a symbol of trust, to then be forced to reconcile the tough reality that they too are capable of committing dishonorable and diabolic criminal acts against humanity.

The ill feeling that the public has when it comes to confronting the reality that police officers commit gruesome criminal acts is very complex and, for some people unfathomable. It is an unease that is akin to the effect that renowned film director Alfred Hitchcock's shower scene in the 1960 thriller *Psycho* had on generations of people, causing them to experience an irrational sense of fear and unease while showering in the safety of their homes. For many people, the apprehension related to associating law enforcement professionals with dastardly deeds can be difficult to deal with.

Policophobia, or the fear of police, can take different forms. For example, in a 1995 *New York Times* article, writer Don Wallace describe his fear of police this way: "Once, when I was sitting with black friends at a crowded basketball game two police officers waded into the bleachers and hauled me out to the floor to be searched, in full view of my teachers and friends. That I was a football player in my letterman's jacket and president of the student body made no difference to the race-baiters in blue; it was probably why I'd been chosen in the first place."[18]

JACK D. McCULLOUGH

Shocking crimes carried out by police officers like those committed by Valle, Peterson, and Dorner are hardly new to the criminal justice system. In a case going back to 1957, a Sycamore, Illinois, family and community had been scarred by the kidnapping and murder of seven-year-old Maria Ridulph for more than a half-century. The crime is considered by criminologists to be the oldest solved cold case in U.S. history. At the time of the girl's murder, the case so alarmed the American public that federal law enforcement officers were sent to the rural Illinois town to investigate. The Ridulph case also garnered the personal attention of FBI chief J. Edgar Hoover.

Jack McCullough, a former police officer in Washington State, was then known as John Tessier, who was at the time of the girl's disappearance 17 years old. After law enforcement had interviewed hundreds of people, including Tessier, the case went cold. The boy went about his life until over a half-century later, when Tessier, now known as Jack D. McCullough and a former neighbor of the girl, was tried and convicted of kidnapping and stabbing Ridulph to death.

A short time after the girl's disappearance, McCullough enlisted in the military and would go on to serve in Southeast Asia. During his military service, McCullough received a Bronze Star for bravery in combat. In the intervening years, McCullough became a police officer and also served as a security guard. It was not until 2008 when McCullough's youngest sister, Janet McCullough, informed the Illinois State Police of what her dying mother had said to her years earlier: "John did it. John did it, and you have to tell someone."[19]

Based on the statement of McCullough's sister, and the fact that his original alibi had fallen apart, the Ridulph case was reopened, and the former police officer, now 71 years old, was finally brought to trial for the girl's murder. McCullough was also charged with committing two sex crimes between 1961 and 1962; his alleged victim was a 14-year-old Sycamore girl. McCullough would be acquitted of the rape, but almost 54 years after the crime, he was sentenced to 33 years in prison for murdering his seven-year-old neighbor.

The emotional impact on the Ridulph family, and residents of the small community, over more than a half-century later, was to say the least extremely hard. When asking the court to impose the maximum sentence allowable on McCullough, Assistant DeKalb County state's attorney Victor Escarcida said, "Jack McCullough left a lifetime of emotional wreckage in his wake."

The girl's brother, Charles Ridulph, said after McCullough's sentencing that his parents, who had lived well into their 90s, never got over their daughter's murder. "All their lives they longed to be with their little daughter," Ridulph wrote in a victim impact statement. "My mother, only days before her death, had a dream, a vision perhaps of being in heaven with Maria."[20]

While McCullough was not a police officer when the child was murdered, still it is chilling to consider that he possessed the capacity to commit such a heinous crime and later take an oath to serve and protect. It is also extremely distressing that, in spite of rigorous screening for psychological fitness performed by police departments nationwide, there are individuals like McCullough who now serve as police officers. Like McCullough, the public depends on them to patrol communities and to keep us safe. Yet, the truth is that some are capable of committing abhorrent acts like the one committed by McCullough.

It must be said that America's law enforcement agencies are mostly comprised of honest and dedicated police officers. However, if we are to increase the quality of personnel in our law enforcement organizations, we must come to terms with the realization that individuals like McCullough, Dorner, Peterson, and Valle were once considered to be honest and dedicated members of the law enforcement community. Though unsettling and difficult to acknowledge, they very likely represent the tip of the iceberg of the police officers that have the capacity to harm innocent people and to smear the reputation of the criminal justice system. Law enforcement officials, politicians, and the public continue to grapple with the effect that police misconduct and criminality has on society. Therefore, it is good to know that a collaborative effort is underway to improve methods of detecting and weeding out individuals with a proclivity to commit crimes, and to violate their sworn oath.

NOTES

1. "Richard J. Daley," http://www.u-s-history.com/pages/h2013.html (accessed March 12, 2013).

2. John Kass, "Hanhardt Walks on New Landscape, but It's the Same Chicago Way," *Chicago Tribune*, July 20, 2011, http://articles.chicago tribune.com/2011-07-20/news/ct-met-kass-0720-20110720_1_bill-hanhardt -hanhardt-friend-federal-prison (accessed April 9, 2013).

3. Bridget Freeland, "Another Black Eye for Chicago Police," *Courthouse News Service*, March 3, 2011, http://www.courthousenews.com/2011/03/03/34620.htm (accessed April 8, 2013).

4. Hall Dardick and John Byrne, *Chicago Tribune*, September 12. 2013.

5. John Knefel, "Bad Cop: 7 Cities Where Shocking Police Abuses Cost Taxpayers Millions," *AlterNet,* March 4, 2013, http://www.alternet.org/civil-liberties/bad-cop-7-cities-where-shocking-police-abuses-cost-taxpayers-millions (accessed July 3, 2014).

6. John Conroy, "Deaf to the Screams," *Chicago Reader*, July 31, 2003, http://www.chicagoreader.com/chicago/deaf-to-the-screams/Content?oid=912813 (accessed April 12, 2013).

7. Todd Lighty and Matt O'Connor, "Rogue Cop Gets Life," *Chicago Tribune*, January 25, 2003, http://articles.chicagotribune.com/2003-01-25/news/0301250139_1_joseph-miedzianowski-gang-members-badge (accessed April 10, 2013).

8. Casey Gane-McCalla, "The Top Five Most Corrupt Police Officers of All-Time." *NewsOne for Black America*, September 28, 2011. http://newsone.com/1551885/top-5-corrupt-police-officers/ (accessed October 22, 2014).

9. "A Brief History of the Boston P.D.—the Oldest Police Dept." http://www.democraticunderground.com/10022722823 (accessed October 31, 2014).

10. The Volstead Act, http://www2.potsdam.edu/hansondj/Controversies/Volstead-Act.html (accessed April 12, 2013).

11. Stephan Benzkofer, "Legendary Lawmen: Part 5—Frank Loesch," *Chicago Tribune*, December 18, 2011, http://articles.chicagotribune.com/2011-12-18/site/ct-per-flash-lawmen-loesch-1218-20111218_1_al-capone-special-prosecutor-public-corruption (accessed March 12, 2013).

12. "Statement by Frank J. Loesch," Schaffer Library of Drug Policy, http://druglibrary.net/schaffer/Library/studies/wick/loesch.htm (accessed April 2, 2013).

13. "Frank Serpico Quotes," http://thinkexist.com/quotes/frank_serpico/ (accessed April 2, 2013).

14. U.S. Attorney Preet Bharara, quoted in Larry Neumeister, "New York's 'Cannibal Cop' Convicted by Federal Jury," *Los Angeles Times*, March 12, 2013, http://www.latimes.com/news/nation/nationnow/la-na-nn-jury-convicts-ny-cannibal-cop-20130312,0,4104363.story (accessed March 12, 2013).

15. Will County States Attorney James Glasgow, quoted in Kennedy Ryan, "Drew Peterson Screams, 'I Did Not Kill Kathleen,' Gets 38 Years,"

KTLA.com, http://ktla.com/2013/02/21/drew-peterson-screams-i-did-not
-kill-kathleen-gets-38-years/#axzz2PGWYY0FR (accessed April 1, 2013).

16. LAPD Chief Charlie Beck, quoted in "Was 'Killer' Ex-Cop Right
about His Firing?" *Daily Mail*, February 10, 2013, http://www.daily
mail.co.uk/news/article-2276475/Christopher-Dorner-LAPD-reopens
-investigation-ex-cops-2009-firing.html#ixzz2PQG4eKgc (accessed April 3,
2013).

17. Diane Wetendorf, "The Impact of Police-Perpetrated Domestic
Violence," http://www.abuseofpower.info/Article_FBI.htm (accessed
April 6, 2013).

18. Don Wallace, "How I Learned to Fear the Cops," *New York Times*,
October 11, 1995, http://www.nytimes.com/1995/10/11/opinion/how-i
-learned-to-fear-the-cops.html (accessed April 15, 2013).

19. Ann O'Neill, "Life Sentence Closes Oldest Cold Case," CNN,
December 11, 2012, http://www.cnn.com/2012/12/10/justice/oldest-cold
-case-sentencing (accessed April 15, 2013).

20. Clifford Ward, "Defiant Ex-Cop Gets Life for Girl's 1957 Murder,"
Chicago Tribune, December 11, 2012, http://articles.chicagotribune.com/
2012-12-11/news/ct-met-mccullough-murder-sentencing-20121211_1
_maria-ridulph-janet-tessier-johnny-and-maria (accessed April 4, 2013).

3

❖

Power, Politics, and Racism

"The art of the police consists in punishing rarely and severely."[1]

JON GRAHAM BURGE'S REIGN OF TERROR

In this chapter, the influence of political ambition, racism, and power and how, together, or as single factors, they can lead to police misconduct and brutality are explored. The overwhelming abundance of allegations against police officers as it relates to misconduct and the use of excessive force against the public are disconcerting to the average citizen. Making matters worse is the fact that a conspiracy to conceal viciousness, as was proven in a court of law against former Chicago Police commander Jon Graham Burge, is not an isolated incident. That said, for advocates of police reform and law enforcement watchdog organizations, Burge is a barefaced example of what is perceived as a system-wide problem, pervasive in nature in police departments throughout the country.

Burge, the former Chicago detective and notorious convicted felon, was accused, indicted, and convicted of ordering and then concealing the torturing of scores of suspects in order to obtain confessions. He is one of many former and active-duty police officers charged with committing similar acts. An examination of Burge's actions points out the critical role that power, politics, and racism play at the front end of our criminal justice system. The charges against Burge, who was sentenced in 2011 to four and a half years in federal prison for lying to a federal grand jury, stands as a terrifying example of what happens when power, politics and racism come together, creating havoc, and bringing nightmarish situations into the lives the innocent. In the end, Burge's actions unfairly exposed hundreds of criminal suspects, their families, and communities to the dark side of law enforcement. Moreover, it brought scandal, dishonor, and public suspicion on the whole of hardworking CPD personnel and the entire Cook County criminal justice system.

The trickle-down effect of the initial accusations against Burge by criminal suspects would ultimately taint the political careers of others. However, others allegedly involved in the outrage escaped ruin. One that has managed to evade the issue for nearly three decades is the then Cook County state's attorney, Richard M. Daley, who is said to have been a close friend of Burge. Daley would go on to become Chicago's longest-serving mayor, remaining in office for 22 years and overtaking the record once held by his father, Richard J. Daley. While Richard M. Daley never faced official charges, and there is nothing to directly connect him to the misdeeds of Burge, even now Daley is haunted by rumors of being complicit in a criminal cover-up related to Burge's horrendous brutality and torturing of criminal suspects. Moreover, after many years of legal wrangling, when Burge was finally indicted, still Daley was not called to testify in the government's case against the former police commander. However, Daley has not been successful in escaping the scrutiny of an increasingly suspicious public, many who believe it implausible that during Daley's tenure as state's attorney, the highest law enforcement official in Cook County, from 1980 until becoming mayor in 1988, could have been completely unaware of the acts ordered or perpetrated by Burge. In spite of this, Daley's supporters consistently counter by saying that the politically astute Daley would have understood the ramifications of participating in a criminal conspiracy to his political career, and thus dismiss the suspicions as absurd. In addition, they assert that Daley had nothing to gain by participating in Burge's conspiracy, and as an adept politician hailing from one of the nation's most powerful and well-known political dynasties, Daley would have never considered taking part in a cover-up of Burge's monstrous acts.

Nonetheless, over a quarter of a century later, in 2012, U.S. District Court judge Rebecca Pallmeyer ruled that Chicago's former law-and-order mayor could be named as a defendant in a civil case brought by plaintiff Michael Tillman, one of the men who alleged being tortured during Burge's decades-long period of criminal activity. Later in this chapter there will be more about Tillman, who says his confession for a 1986 rape and murder for which he served 24 years in prison was coerced through physical torture ordered by Burge and carried out by Chicago police officers. In 2010, Tillman was vindicated of the crime when the court ruled in his favor, vacating the conviction.

Chicago politics during the early 1980s, coupled with Daley's shaky political position, were entirely different from what they had been when Daley's father ruled the city—some say with an iron fist—from 1955 until his death in 1976. One thing that's certain is that by the time Richard M. Daley became mayor, the days of supreme rule were at an end. Still, during the time that Daley served as state's attorney, the "Chicago Way" was also undergoing tremendous change, and was far and away from what it had been under his father's two-decade-long rule as mayor. The father ran a synchronized well-oiled political machine, one in which the existence of independents or political adversaries to the machine were for all practical purposes nonexistent, bordering on extinction, or annihilated.

In the early 1980s, Chicago was rife with political and racial discord and literally in the throes of what writer Steve Chapman described with exacting frankness: "In the 1980s, Chicago politics were a bubbling cauldron of racial antagonisms. Harold Washington won in 1983 by mobilizing black voters, who were resentful of their treatment by the white mayor, Jane Byrne, and hungry to gain a new role at City Hall."[2] Chapman is referring to a contentious three-way Democratic mayoral primary between mayoral incumbent Byrne, Richard M. Daley, and U.S. Representative Harold Washington. In the end Washington went on to become Chicago's first African American mayor, ushering in an era remembered as anything but calmness and racial harmony. Instead, it is recalled for the ratcheting of divisiveness and racially charged politics that lasted until Washington's untimely death in 1987.

It is widely held that Washington's 1983 victory was, in a number of ways, pivotal to Daley's success and political future. For one thing, Daley had to have known that if another opportunity to run for mayor came his way, his success would hinge on a record of successful prosecutions as Cook County state's attorney. Daley's record as a law-and-order candidate would be the platform of his mayoral run, and as a shrewd politician whose family had been in public service for decades and was synonymous with Chicago politics, Daley took an important lesson from his primary defeat to Washington, which was to not take African American voters for granted. Knowing that blacks had voted overwhelming to elect Washington, giving him a whopping 99 percent of their vote, with Hispanic voters following closely behind with 82 percent, it was a safe bet that Daley would court the minority vote early, and that he would be exceedingly careful not to alienate blacks by not taking their concerns seriously.

Yet, it was a tightrope for Daley, who since his time as state's attorney had prosecuted many of the black men tortured with Burge's consent, and who would later tell their stories of the unspeakable horrors they endured. The question that was being asked by some onlookers was what Daley knew about Burge's misconduct, and if so, when he knew about it. If Daley's record of convictions as state's attorney was linked to the atrocities committed under Burge, the effect on Daley's popularity and his mayoral prospect would have been disastrous. Yet, on the other hand, if Daley was viewed as a state's attorney who was doing his job by taking dangerous criminals off the streets, the black community would applaud his effort and likely bestow on him the same support that they did his father, helping elect him to six terms as mayor.

Clearly, as state's attorney, prosecuting criminals was Daley's number-one focus, and he often touted that it was his primary responsibility to the people of Cook County. Like other state's attorneys, Daley's job approval largely depended on a record of effectiveness that was directly connected to the success of the work done by the police officer on the street. Therefore, men like Burge who were counted on to make arrests, and to obtain confessions that would hold up in court and under the scrutiny of the defense attorneys representing the accused, was of the utmost importance to Daley's political aspirations. First and foremost, this meant that criminal evidence could not be tainted by improper search and seizure or illegal arrests, or at risk of being summarily dismissed based on evidence offered by defense attorneys alleging wrongful police conduct.

One way to prevent this from occurring is to obtain a confession from the suspect. An admission of guilt decisively clears hurdles that would otherwise be required by the prosecutor, and thereby reduces the burden on the taxpayers as well as encumbrance on the judicial system. These factors were tremendously important to Daley's political future, and of specific importance were the criminal confessions that would go a long way to demonstrate that, under Daley, the state's attorney's office had been highly effective when going after criminal suspects who were committing crimes and creating havoc in Cook County.

To give an idea of Daley's success and focus on crime as state's attorney, according to *Chicago Magazine*, in 1979 on Daley's predecessor Bernard Carey's watch, over 900 people were prosecuted for felonies charges related to drugs. In 1984, as state's attorney, Daley pressed charges against nearly 4,500 people, five times more than under Carey. Remarkably, Daley, who had never tried a criminal case when he was elected as Cook County state's attorney, also outpaced Carey by winning a phenomenal 82 percent of the court cases brought to jury, over Carey's 78 percent record.

Daley's strict stance on crime, particularly drug offenses, is a matter of public record. According to David Jackson, who interviewed Daley for a 1988 *Chicago Magazine* piece, Daley articulated his position on drugs by succinctly stating that, "To me, a narcotics dealer is the most dangerous person out there. He makes your murderers, your rapists, your home invaders, destroys your kids, your kids will rob from you, they'll steal from you, they'll quit school."[3] Daley's hardened approach on behalf of victims of crime was something that had the potential to affect every facet of law enforcement in Cook County, from the cop on the street to the judges who heard and sentenced an unending procession of criminal defendants that came before them as a result of Daley's crime-fighting crusade. As champion of those whose communities were plagued by drug-related crime and violence, Daley would soon earn praise and widespread support, especially in the black community.

According to Chapman, as state's attorney, Daley's office had a major influence over the criminal courts that affected how the crimes were treated to the way that Cook County judges sentenced the convicted. In spite of the fact that law enforcement professionals, including police officers, criminologists, and judges, said that Daley's uncompromising position on crime did not correlate to a reduction in the number of crimes being committed, an undeterred Daley continued his relentless drive to address almost every incident of crime, with punitive measures aimed at incarcerating criminals. In doing so, Daley's tough-on-crime objective frequently tied the hands of judges that on occasion may have wanted to use their judicial discretion when sentencing some individuals who, for instance, may have benefited from the court's leniency especially if coupled with an appropriate approach of rehabilitation. Dennis Cooley, a supervisor in the Cook County state's attorney's office, resigned during Daley's administration, saying this about the zeal to prosecute all criminal activity during Daley's years as state's attorney, "Reach into a car window and steal a pair of sunglasses and you'll be charged with a felony now—the equivalent of breaking into a bank . . . I don't mind that if it's the only way to catch an Al Capone, but they're doing this to 17-year-old kids."[4]

Cooley's frustration is supported by the fact that despite the incredible increase in the number of arrests, convictions, and strong sentences under Daley, or for that matter any prosecutor, the evidence is scant that it resulted in a reduction in crime. Nonetheless, in Chicago the law-and-order offensive continued, and the courts were inundated with criminal defendants, while the prison system filled to capacity. John Tierney's

2012 *New York Times* story notes that, "Three decades of stricter drug laws, reduced parole and rigid sentencing rules have lengthened prison terms and more than tripled the percentage of Americans behind bars. The United States has the highest reported rate of incarceration of any country: about one in 100 adults, a total of nearly 2.3 million people in prison or jail."[5] Tierney's point that the land of the free and home of the brave has the world's largest prison population makes some people very uncomfortable and causes one to think about what America has come to symbolize. Despite the worrisome statistics, a cavalcade of criminal defendants charged with felonies continues to strain criminal courts throughout the country.

Believed at the time to be entirely within legal bounds, decades later, many of the successful convictions would come back to haunt the individuals who participated in the arrests, interrogations, indictments, and trials connected to Daley's prosecutorial days. As evidence of torture-induced and tainted confessions reverberated throughout the Cook County court system, the long road to indict Burge and those under his lengthy run as a Chicago police commander began. Eventually, many successful criminal convictions occurring during Daley's time as state's attorney would be overturned, and at a huge cost to taxpayers. Not to mention the human toll, and the many lives altered, as a result of the police misconduct and brutality that has been validated and is now a matter of public record.

From this, one begins to get an idea of how crucial criminal prosecutions were to Daley's political ambitions, as well as the role that they would continue to play in taking him to six consecutive terms as Chicago's mayor. However, this was not only important to Daley's political career, but also of great significance to prosecutors throughout the country, especially to those who then and now rely on a record of successful criminal convictions to advance their own political careers; and to the individuals whose personal and professional relationship with Daley could directly impact their own careers, be it in politics or other pursuits. Therefore, it is reasonable to conclude that they understood exactly how their futures were connected to Daley's success, as well as the risks associated with riding the coattails of a politician. This of course includes Burge, whose rise through the ranks of the Chicago Police Department was primarily propelled by the criminal arrests and confessions obtained during the Daley era. It stands to reason that Burge would have been keenly aware of the clear-cut effect that criminal arrests, interrogations, and resulting criminal confessions and successful convictions would have on Daley's political future and rise to power. Moreover, it is not a stretch to conclude that Burge deduced that his own ambitions were directly connected to Daley's.

While this does not necessarily equate to indisputable proof that as state's attorney, Daley knew about Burge's malevolent activities, it does lend powerful circumstantial weight to those who imply that Daley must have been aware of it, because it so plainly impacted his political career, and particularly his aspiration to run again as mayor of Chicago. What is absolutely certain is that the integrity of the arrests and convictions during Daley's time as state's attorney was enormously important not only to Daley, but also to people who worked in the state's attorney's office and to members of the Chicago Police Department, including Burge. It is also obvious that Daley's political adversaries and would-be opponents were marginalized by the success of the state's attorney office under Daley.

For instance, the impact that Daley's onslaught against crime would have had on the rank-and-file police officers responsible for patrolling the streets of Chicago and making routine criminal arrests was immense. Police officers were, after all, on the front lines combating all manner of criminal activity, including the menaces of gangs and drugs. While the affect was not instantly detectable, it should be noted that as early as 1972 and during Daley's father's time in power, some four years before his son began serving as state's attorney, rumors were circulating regarding a crew of police intimidators that, under Burge's command, were using coercion, torture, and other forms of brute force and intimidation to obtain confessions from criminal suspects.

It's well documented that the black community's relationship with Chicago police officers and law enforcement organizations had been deteriorating for years. As the incidence of police brutality and misconduct grew routine, particularly in the black community, so did the skepticism and distrust by many blacks toward Chicago police officers. Yet, it was an incident in 1969 that is seen as a turning point in the black community's relationship with Chicago police officers, and the Cook County state's attorney's office specifically, as proof positive for some blacks that the state attorney's office under Edward V. Hanrahan, the then state's attorney, and the criminal justice system hierarchy were in cahoots against the black community and its leaders. Moreover, the 1969 incident is believed by many to have been a turning point, setting the tone for the police brutality and pervasive misconduct that occurred on Daley's watch, and under Burge's command.

Four decades later, Chicagoans continue to examine the politics and circumstances that lead to the killing of Black Panther leaders Fred Hampton and Mark Clark. The men were killed during a predawn raid carried out by the Cook County state's Attorney's office, with the backing of the CPD. However, it is Hampton, a black man barely in his 20s, who was able to rouse the highest levels of Chicago's body politic and the law enforcement community to what some believe resulted in the conniving and carrying out of a cold-blooded murder.

According to his followers, Hampton was a phenomenal grassroots organizer and exceedingly deft at getting under the skin of Chicago's powerful boss, Mayor Richard J. Daley. Hampton also recognized, very astutely, that Chicago's poor had grown tired of the gratuitous Christmas turkeys and glad tidings sent down from City Hall to assuage the downtrodden. Hampton also saw that a large segment of Chicago's disadvantaged were ready to join the battle against capitalism and racism emanating from City Hall and beyond. Wise beyond his years, the Illinois Black Panther chairman had figured out that by bringing blacks, Latinos, and poor whites together to form a "Rainbow Coalition," comprised of the long-suffering and ignored impoverished populations, could result in a collective coalescing around the common goal of working together against a powerful exclusionary class system that was stacked against them. This political strategy at first only mildly irritated Mayor Daley; however, as time passed and the impact of Hampton's plan came to fruition, it would consume and infuriate Daley.

From the beginning, Hampton and the Black Panthers had advanced a controversial and revolutionary doctrine that was completely the opposite of Dr. Martin Luther King's code of nonviolence. Hampton's idea to dare the underclass to seize the momentum of change that was prevalent in the 1960s, and to take control of their destiny, appealed to the younger oppressed masses. This was particularly true on Chicago's South and West Sides, where young black men discovered in Hampton's audaciousness a vision of something different from what their fathers had dared to imagine. Many felt that what Hampton and the Panthers were doing transcended anything done before in Black America, and they perceived that the battle cry for Black Power represented not only something different, but the embodiment of a drastic alternative to the passé nonviolent ideology that their parents had remained faithful to, yet had little to show for their allegiance.

Nevertheless, standing in opposition to the Panthers was the political and law enforcement power structure that simply could not fathom the incendiary premise of self-reliance and Black Power espoused by the Panthers. To those who occupied the seat of power, the idea that black people had the nerve to express confidence in themselves and to believe that they should defend themselves against their oppressors was viewed as obscene, threatening, and insufferable. In Chicago, and in urban centers across America, as the Black Panthers' message resonated in minority communities, Mayor Richard J. Daley's ire, and that of other elected officials and heads of law enforcement, intensified.

In 1968 in the days following Martin Luther King's assassination, when rioting broke out in Chicago, Mayor Daley took the looting and firing of buildings and businesses as a personal affront. As the rioting, arson, and looting spread, Daley issued his infamous order to Chicago police "to shoot to kill any arsonist or anyone with a Molotov cocktail in his hand . . . and . . . to shoot to maim or cripple anyone looting any stores in our city."[6] Daley's outrageous and incredibly contentious command divided Chicagoans along racial lines. Many whites believed that the mayor's order was necessary, while to an overwhelming majority of blacks, the directive was perceived as extreme, blatantly racist, and a monumental political blunder. There is no doubt that Daley's shoot-to-kill order added to the growing list of insults that outraged poor blacks, furthering their suspicion of Daley and his political ally, Cook County state's attorney Hanrahan.

Meanwhile, in the wake of Dr. King's death and amid the mounting dissatisfaction and racial turmoil, in impoverished South and West Side Chicago neighborhoods, Hampton's charismatic leadership was winning the hearts and minds of the underprivileged and disenfranchised. Offering what no African American leader had before, Hampton reached out to oppressed and reformist-minded blacks, captivating them with provocative talk about giving power to the people. By the end of 1968, the Chicago chapter of the Black Panthers was attracting scores of new recruits by utilizing a brilliantly balanced message augmented by tangible programs to fight hunger, eliminate poor housing conditions, and the centerpiece, putting an end to police brutality.

The Panthers' strategy seemed to be working, galvanizing blacks around issues related to self-defense and reliance. As Hampton's reputation and legend grew, so did the attention of federal and local law enforcement authorities, which shunned the Panthers' doctrine by launching a propaganda campaign aimed at defining the Panthers as violent extremists. In order to counter Hampton's growing notoriety and to tarnish the Panthers' reputation, in 1969, Hanrahan ordered three raids on Black Panther properties, which resulted in negative publicity and hundreds of arrests. However, Hanrahan's actions also increased suspicion among blacks toward the state's attorney office and the CPD. In fact, Hampton's supporters generally viewed the raids as organized political harassment initiated by Mayor Daley, whose strategy, they believed, was aimed at bringing an end to the Panthers' presence in Chicago. Future attempts to do just that were expanded to a consortium of government agencies whose sole purpose was believed to have been to obliterate the burgeoning Black Panther presence in Chicago.

The relentless determination of law enforcement to take action against Hampton and the Panthers reached critical mass when the Cook County state's attorney's office and officers assigned to the CPD captured national attention on December 4, 1969. Hanrahan, who had been a protégé of Daley and rumored as a possible successor to the mayor, ordered a raid on the headquarters and residence of the Chicago Black Panther Party. At the time of the raid, and enduring over four decades later, is the common belief that the police action was a culmination of political ambition, racism, and fear. Clearly, the assault on a chilly December morning in 1969 was indicative of the volatile political and racist environment that existed in Chicago, and one in which an assault on the Panthers' headquarters was deemed to be an appropriate response, by a myriad of law enforcement agency professionals and Cook County's criminal justice system.

In the predawn hours, law enforcement officers equipped with a floor plan that had been provided by an FBI informant fired over 100 bullets into the Panthers' headquarters. Black Panthers Hampton and Mark Clark were killed during the raid. According to official autopsy reports, Hampton was shot twice in the head at point-blank range. Word quickly spread throughout the black community that one police officer who participated in the raid was heard to have said, "He's good and dead now."[7] Suspicion aimed at Harahan's office and the CPD hierarchy spread like wildfire, increasing the chasm of distrust toward local law enforcement by blacks, one that prevails decades later.

In 1969, I was an impressionable teenager, who by chance arrived at the scene of the killing of Hampton and Clark just hours after the incident. Several years ago, I recalled the incident and what I'd witnessed that morning in my weekly column, on the 41st anniversary of their deaths, pinpointing to the exact hour when my racial consciousness was transformed. For a number of years, the incident shaped my feelings about law enforcement, as I am certain it did for many in the black community who felt subjugated by law enforcement and reluctant to interact with police officers. In fact, it was widely held by many blacks that the Panthers' progressive message had so resonated in the black community, and that their boldness was so troubling to politicians and the criminal justice system, that nothing short of their total annihilation was considered by the establishment. While we may never know, what is clear is that the hail of bullets that brought to an abrupt end what is believed to have been the most definitive movement of black unity and self-sufficiency in

Chicago's impoverished communities was replaced by distrust of law enforcement organizations that lead to decades of police misconduct and brutality the likes of which Chicago—and, for that matter, America— had up until then not witnessed.

JON BURGE

After graduating from high school, Burge enlisted in the army. During his time in the military, he received two commendations for valor. The commendations were awarded for dragging a wounded comrade to safety while under fire. Burge's military record was beyond reproach, and the U.S. Army veteran, attached to the military police, was stationed in South Korea and Vietnam, where he volunteered his service. Burge was honorably discharged in 1969, and he started his career as a Chicago police officer in 1970, at the age of 22. Early in his law enforcement career, Burge started racking up various commendations and began his ascent through the ranks of the CPD.

There is absolutely nothing in Burge's military record to suggest that he participated in acts that would portend the misconduct that he participated in as a CPD police commander. In fact, according to the *Chicago Sun-Times*, Burge's legal team sought to use the disgraced cop's exemplary military record when seeking a shorter prison term, following the guilty verdict handed down for three counts of obstruction of justice and perjuring himself in federal court.

Oddly, the allegations against Burge and a squad of Chicago cops who worked for him, dubbed the "Midnight Crew" and also implicated in intimidating and torturing black criminal suspects, were common knowledge to some individuals in law enforcement and criminal circles. For years, criminal suspects had complained, though unsuccessfully, about the intimidation and methods of torture used by Chicago police officers to obtain false criminal confessions. However, the accusations of police misconduct were not taken seriously until, in an ironic twist, a persistent convicted cop killer with an IQ of 78, who couldn't read and had not graduated from elementary school, initiated a prolonged legal fight to expose Burge's sadistic criminal behavior and misuse of police powers.

Andrew Wilson and his brother Jackie, who were convicted in the 1982 killing of Chicago police officers William Fahey and Richard O'Brien, would play a pivotal role in bringing to light the sinister acts being perpetrated by Burge and others within the CPD. When Andrew Wilson fingered Burge in a civil lawsuit, it opened the floodgates for claims against the city of Chicago, claims that would continue years after Wilson's 2007 death while imprisoned. Dozens of former criminal suspects, who were black men, came forth alleging torture by Burge's Midnight Crew. In a number of cases, previously rendered guilty verdicts were reversed, and the confessions of the wrongly convicted were deemed to have been coerced through acts of torture at the hands of Burge and his crew.

In addition, Cook County taxpayers had to and continue to pay millions of dollars in settlements related to years of police misconduct and brutality, corroborated by eyewitness accounts, committed under Burge's command. As the individuals claiming mistreatment by Chicago police officers have continued to come forward alleging mistreatment, their numbers so great, it appeared to some that the litigation was headed toward class-action status. However, in March 2014, a Cook County judge ruled that "imprisoned men who say they were tortured by Chicago Police Cmdr. Jon Burge and his subordinates can't pursue a class-action lawsuit."[8] So, instead of a class-action lawsuit, something that many thought to be the best way to deal with the steady stream of allegations piling up against Burge and the CPD, the court assigned Loyola University Law School dean David Yellen to ascertain the legitimacy of claims made by men incarcerated during Burge's rule.

According to John Conroy, a Chicago writer who has chronicled the Burge story since the early 1990s, the Wilson brothers' incident began in 1982 when Andrew, masquerading as a postman, burglarized a home on Chicago's South Side. When the homeowner, Leveda Downs, opened the door to receive what she believed to be an authentic delivery, Andrew pulled a gun and the brothers forced their way inside, tying the woman up and looting her home.

By chance the crime occurred just blocks from where I lived at the time, on Chicago's South Side. I recall first hearing what seemed like the non-stop piercing sound of police sirens, followed by a blitz of police vehicles surrounding the area. Within a matter of minutes, the neighborhood was teeming with police activity. Word quickly spread that there had been a shooting and that the victims were two Chicago police officers who were later identified as William Fahey and Richard O'Brien. Sections of the community were cordoned off, and residents were gripped with fear. Passions ran high as police conducted a door-to-door manhunt to apprehend the individual responsible for killing the officers.

As rumors of Chicago police officers physically knocking down doors, terrorizing residents, and shooting pets spread, so did ill feelings toward the CPD. It is also true that the action taken by Chicago police officers in the aftermath of the gunning down of Fahey and O'Brien, and during the hunt for their killers, added to mounting racial tension and alienation of the black community. As a result, a number of black leaders protested, saying that the CPD's tactics and fervor to catch the perpetrators of the crime had amounted to racism and an unofficial declaration of martial law in the black community. One prominent spokesperson, Afro-American Police League director Renault Robinson, referred to the search for the Wilson Brothers as "sloppy police work, a matter of racism." Chiming in, Reverend Jesse Jackson declared that the black community was in "a war zone . . . under economic, political, and military occupation," and that the CPD was holding "the entire black community hostage for the crimes of two."[9] This sentiment was shared not only by African American leaders, but by many who resided in minority neighborhoods throughout the city.

However, to grasp the viewpoint of Auburn Gresham residents and that of the law enforcement community at the time of the hunt for the Wilson brothers, it helps to have an understanding of the racial history of the community and what was going on at the time of the shooting. The *Encyclopedia of Chicago* indicates that during the 1960s in the area of the city known as Auburn Gresham, where officers Fahey and O'Brien were gunned down, crime rose at a rate faster than in Chicago as a whole. During the same period, Chicago was an ethnically segregated city. It is also worth noting that over four decades later, according to the Manhattan Institute for Policy Research, the city is still considered to be the most segregated in the nation.

In 1966, at the height of the civil rights struggle, racial volatility was intense across America as the fight for civil rights was at a fever pitch. In Chicago, some residents of Marquette Park, a white community not far from Auburn Gresham, threw rocks at Dr. Martin Luther King Jr. during a civil rights march. By 1970, Auburn Gresham was 69 percent black, and in 1982 when officers Fahey and O'Brien were shot to death, in just over a month, five law enforcement officers had been wounded, four fatally. Among them were two deputy sheriffs, who were shot during an armed robbery, and rookie police officer James Doyle, who was killed when arresting a robbery suspect. Needless to say, Auburn Gresham residents and members of the law enforcement community were on edge, and rightfully so. Moreover, the personal beliefs of some elected officials and law enforcement professionals, coupled with public demand and political pressure to take the cop killers into custody, intensified. It is also true that the careers of numerous law enforcement professionals hinged on the swift apprehension of the cop killers, including Burge's. In fact, accused cop killer Wilson would later testify that during his interrogation into the murders of Fahey and O'Brien, Burge would say, "My reputation is at stake and you are going to make a statement."[10]

In an article recounting the events immediately following the killing of Fahey and O'Brien, John Conroy wrote that at the time, "Lieutenant Jon Burge, commanding officer of Area 2 Violent Crimes, was off duty when the incident occurred. He was at a car wash at 87th and Langley when a detective came running through looking for the suspect vehicle. The detective told Burge of the shootings, and almost simultaneously Burge's beeper went off. He sped to his office to take charge of the investigation. He would not return home for five days."[11] After chasing several leads, on Valentine's Day, Burge personally arrested Andrew Wilson without incident.

However, the slaying of Fahey and O'Brien is not where the saga of atrocities committed by and under the direction of Burge begins. Claims like those made by Wilson that Burge and other police officers used electrical shock, a cigarette, and a radiator to burn him, punched him, and placed a plastic bag over his head, preventing him from breathing, while alarming and to some unbelievable, were proven to be the modus operandi documented by simultaneous medical reports and photographic proof. In fact, long before Wilson's $10 million lawsuit, CPD officers were said to have elicited confessions from criminal suspects by using brutal physical mistreatment, including the inhumane torture alleged by Wilson. Allegations made by criminal suspects other than Wilson naming Burge as their torturer and the telling of stories related to police officers using abusive means in order to obtain confessions were commonplace. There are also accounts of Chicago police officers setting up criminal suspects with drugs and illegal firearms, a ploy routinely used to bring about criminal confessions.

In one case, a criminal suspect named Anthony Holmes alleged that Burge had used electrical shock on him in 1973. Another man, Michael Johnson, had filed a complaint alleging that Burge had used electrical shock on his testicles. Still another, George Powell, claimed that Burge had used a cattle prod to shock him in the chest and stomach. Conroy tells of other men who describe their treatment at the hand of officers assigned to Burge, men like Gregory Banks, who claimed that detectives beat him with a flashlight and put a gun in his mouth, saying that, "they had something special reserved for niggers."[12] Because the officers involved had been accused of using similar methods to interrogate other criminal suspects, the Illinois Appellate Court ordered a retrial for Banks.

The mounting accusations of police misconduct, excessive force, and brutality would over time further damage the already tenuous relationship and increase the chasm between Chicago police officers and residents of the black community. Another unfortunate consequence of the distrust created by the brutality initiated by Burge and others was the reverberation in minority communities, where wariness toward police officers was being transformed into animosity. Today, the aftereffect of police misconduct, excessive force, and brutality playing out in urban communities across the country contributes to a phenomenon in contemporary black culture known as "snitching." Considered taboo by many, "snitching" describes the irrational prohibition against betraying the black race by providing information to law enforcement officials related to alleged criminal activities committed by minorities. The derogatory labeling of those who snitch is perceived as a consequence of the mistreatment of criminal suspects by police officers during interrogations like those carried out with Burge's consent. Throughout urban America, police and the criminal justice system are in some cases legitimately viewed as the enemy and believed participants in a conspiracy to keep minorities incarcerated for a number of reasons, including to feed the prison-industrial complex. This widely held opinion of police officers is reinforced by the actions of individuals who utilize unlawful and malicious behavior toward minority criminal suspects, and it is viewed as being dogmatic, systemic, and condoned by the upper echelon of law enforcement. The belief that police officers are given the go-ahead to execute suspects, white or black, for shooting or killing a law enforcement officer is not far-fetched. While it is generally unspoken, members of the law enforcement community are known to believe it to be equitable payback. If arrangements to surrender are not made and somehow publicly announced, the perpetrators are not likely to make it to the police station and are often killed by the police.

However, in the case of the Wilson brothers, both were apprehended, brought to trial, and convicted of their crimes. Andrew was convicted of both murders, and his brother Jackie of one. The two were sentenced to life in prison without the possibility of parole. However, from prison, the Wilson brothers did not simply go away to serve their life sentences and instead, in 1983, filed lawsuits alleging that they had been beaten and tortured during the interrogation for the crimes that they were later convicted of committing. The suit brought by Andrew Wilson named, besides Burge, former police superintendent Richard Brzeczek and four Chicago police detectives. Yet, it was obvious that Burge in his role as commander of the other officers, who carried out the vicious acts of brutality, would be viewed as the primary offender.

Advocates for the tortured men contend that the vigorous legal defense for Burge, whose name is synonymous with the most heinous police brutality in the history of the CPD, along with the officers who participated in the cruelties were in fact to protect Richard M. Daley's political future.

There was and continues to be speculation that if Daley, as the highest-ranking elected law enforcement official in Cook County, knew about Burge's activities, he would have been complicit in a conspiracy. This would of course have derailed his political aspirations, as well as the future of the individuals close to him. This is a rational assumption given that defenders of the Wilson brothers argued convincingly that Wilson had told the chief of the felony review section, Larry Hyman, that Burge and members of his Midnight Crew had tortured him. Yet, during Wilson's confession and in the presence of a court reporter, Hyman failed to ask the obvious question regarding whether Wilson's statement had been given voluntarily. Prompting further speculation, if nothing else, Hyman's failure to mention it was a gross oversight that should have stirred then Cook County state's attorney Richard Daley or his first assistant Dick Devine to probe deeper into the situation. However, there is no record of inquiry to indicate that this was done, and Daley has denied in federal court records that he knew anything about the Burge's evil cabal of men who tortured criminal suspects.

Still, over the years, the investigation and litigation related to the torture allegations continue, as have Burge's legal fees, now said to be in the millions and paid in part by the Chicago Police Union and taxpayer dollars. However, things started to change for Burge—and, in the opinion of some, to unravel—as a result of the perseverance of claims made by Wilson and his attorneys from the People's Law Office. In the end, the court awarded Wilson a substantial judgment of $50,000 in compensatory damages and $400,000 for attorney fees.

Following Burge's firing from the police department in 1993, and his subsequent 2010 conviction for lying under oath in a civil case about the torture of criminal suspects, many more individuals alleging being beaten and tortured by police officers have come forward to bring lawsuits against the city of Chicago. In some cases, sentences were reversed and huge settlements paid to those wrongly incarcerated. In addition, the pressure to question Daley was ramped up after his 2011 retirement from politics. Attempts were restarted to question the former mayor under oath about his knowledge of the events. The renewed effort to depose Daley came when the rape and murder conviction of Michael Tillman, who served 24 years in prison, was thrown out in 2010. Tillman accused Burge's Midnight Crew of beating, burning, and threatening to kill him. Tillman asked that Daley be deposed, and after drawn-out negotiations, Daley agreed. However, after finally consenting to the deposition, according to the *Chicago Tribune*, Daley avoided being questioned when, "Aldermen to-day recommended paying more than $7 million to two men who say they were tortured by former Police Cmdr. Jon Burge, a move that means former Mayor Richard Daley will not be deposed about what he may have known about one of the cases."[13]

In black communities, the cynicism about police officers is based on societal distinctions that to an extent explain their misgivings toward police officers. For example, in black communities, police officers are viewed as having total power over the neighborhoods that they patrol. Police presence is routinely viewed as a military-like occupation. On the other hand, in white communities, the law enforcement mantra to serve and protect is viewed much differently. There is a prevalent belief in the black community that whites are assumed to be law-abiding citizens, unless they are caught in the act of running afoul of the law.

The great American comic and first recipient of the Mark Twain Prize in 1998, Richard Pryor, was known for his poignant social observations and considered everything fair game. Pryor expounded on the difference in the way that whites and blacks interact with police officers, observing that white people have a friendly and easygoing relationship with the police. According to Pryor, whites know police officers as their neighbors and buddies. For example, when they encounter a police officer on the street, they greet them as Officer Smith or Johnson. Whereas, according to Pryor, blacks have an entirely different rapport with the cops. Here Pryor describes the typical black experience with a police officer:

> You wonder why a nigger don't go completely mad. You get your stuff together. You work all week, right? Then you get dressed, right? And you go out and get clean and be driving with your old lady, going out to a club.
>
> And the police pull you over. "Get out of the car. There was a robbery. The nigger looked just like you. All right, put your hands up, take your pants down, and spread your cheeks."
>
> Now, what nigger feel like having fun after that? "No, let's just go home, baby." You go home, beat your kids. You gonna take that crap out on somebody.[14]

Pryor's societal comedic spin remains pretty much on point. It is true that police officers are viewed in a totally different way by many blacks and are for the most part seen as exercising total power over minorities. The police evoke suspicion and fear especially among young minorities, who see the police as a menacing. Discussing the relationship and distrust of police, 17-year-old Travell Jackson said, "Sometimes the police act just like another gang." The police officers that patrol inner-city streets are often walking a fine line between identifying dangerous criminals and being accused of racial profiling and violating someone's civil rights. An unidentified police officer illustrates the paradox, telling the *Chicago Tribune*, "We're dealing with dangerous criminals. When you do identify them, how do you prevent them from committing a crime? You can't stop them every second or you're violating their civil rights. As far as keeping track of their movements, that's virtually impossible, too."[15]

As recently as July 2013, an Illinois state commission found evidence of police torture related to five criminal convictions occurring under Burge. Adding to a cynical public's speculation and suspicion about police misconduct, and the likelihood that it is being covered up, some law enforcement organizations continue to fight to prevent disclosure of the specifics related to incidents of police misconduct during investigations. For instance, in Chicago, Mayor Rahm Emanuel did not give up the legal fight to prevent disclosure of the information until the courts, not once but twice, ruled that, "records of police misconduct complaints are public under the Illinois Freedom of Information Act."[16] The landmark ruling aimed at changing what for Chicago and other municipalities represents a change in what is believed to be connected to systemic misconduct and cover-up, comes after journalist Jamie Kalven's request for records related to a case going back to 2007 alleging physical and sexual misconduct by five CPD officers. And the beat goes on.

NOTES

1. Napoleon Bonaparte, quoted in *Napoleon: Quotations and Commentary*, edited by L. James Hammond, http://www.ljhammond.com/notebook/nap-right.htm (accessed April 15, 2013).

2. Steve Chapman, "For Chicago Mayor, a Race against Race," *Reason*, February 14, 2011, http://reason.com/archives/2011/02/14/for-chicago-mayor-a-race-again (accessed April 15, 2013).

3. David Jackson, "The Law and Richard M. Daley," *Chicago Magazine*, September 1988, http://www.chicagomag.com/Chicago-Magazine/September-1988/The-Law-and-Richard-M-Daley/ (accessed April 15, 2013).

4. Ibid.

5. John Tierney, "For Lesser Crimes, Rethinking Life behind Bars," *New York Times*, December 11, 2012, http://www.nytimes.com/2012/12/12/science/mandatory-prison-sentences-face-growing-skepticism.html?pagewanted=all&_r=0 (accessed April 15, 2013).

6. James Coates, "Riots Follow Killing of Martin Luther King Jr.," *Chicago Tribune*, April 5, 1968, http://www.chicagotribune.com/news/politics/chi-chicagodays-kingriots-story,0,4609945.story (accessed April 28, 2013).

7. Teresa Wiltz, "The Death of Fred Hampton," *Chicago Tribune*, February 20, 1998, http://articles.chicagotribune.com/1998-02-20/features/9802200116_1_illinois-chapter-black-panther-party-young-man (accessed April 17, 2013).

8. "Class Action Lawsuit Denied for Alleged Burge Torture Victims," March 12, 2014, http://www.nbcchicago.com/news/local/Class-Action-Lawsuit-Denied-For-Alleged-Burge-Torture-Victims-249985661.html (accessed May 4, 2014).

9. John Conroy, "House of Screams," *Chicago Reader*, January 28, 1990, http://www.chicagoreader.com/chicago/house-of-screams/Content?oid=875107 (accessed April 18, 2013).

10. Ibid.

11. Ibid.

12. Ibid.

13. John Byrne and Hal Dardick, "City Settles Burge Torture Case, Avoids Daley Deposition," *Chicago Tribune*, July 23, 2012, http://articles.chicagotribune.com/2012-07-23/news/chi-city-settles-burge-torture-case-avoids-daley-deposition-20120723_1_burge-torture-burge-victims-daley-deposition (accessed April 23, 2013).

14. "Richard Pryor: Stand-Up Philosopher," *Spring Journal*, Spring 2009, http://www.city-journal.org/2009/19_2_urb-richard-pryor.html (accessed April 28, 2013).

15. Dawn Turner Trice and Lolly Bowean, "More Police, More Arrests, More Fear," *Chicago Tribune*, April 26, 2013, http://articles.chicagotribune.com/2013-04-26/news/ct-met-chicago-police-distrust-20130426_1_police-corruption-foot-patrols-rogue-cops/2 (accessed April 28, 2013).

16. "Editorial: Prying Open Police Misconduct Files," *Chicago Tribune*, July 15, 2014, http://www.chicagotribune.com/news/opinion/editorials/ct-chicago-police-misconduct-files-edit-20140715-story.html (accessed July 15, 2014).

4

❖

What Makes a Dirty Cop?

"I am the Law."[1]

The age-old question of what makes a dirty cop is a perplexing one that produces equally puzzling responses. Some speculate that corrupt police officers would have eventually demonstrated a proclivity for wrongdoing regardless of their career choice. Others believe that determining what makes a cop dirty or ignites criminal behavior is akin to the proverbial question of which came first, the chicken or the egg. On the other hand, there are some who attribute police officers that engage in criminal activity to the power bestowed to them and an increased opportunity to get away with it, by virtue of their ability to conceal their misdeeds, as well as other advantages that are not accessible to civilians. I believe that it first depends on the individual and how they handle the bringing together of these things, and more.

The theory that merely giving police powers to some people somehow changes the individual—transforming what had been an honest, forthright individual into a person that over time develops feelings of superiority, entitlement, and immunity from the very laws they are sworn to uphold—can't be easily dismissed. However, it does not explain officers who have unblemished careers and are never tempted to cross the line. Naturally, there are many other hypotheses related to police corruption and misconduct, some that point-blank connect the misuse of power, brutality, and crimes of opportunity to preexisting character flaws that are rooted in a predisposition to behave dishonorably.

Nonetheless, the cold truth is that the people who work in law enforcement are comprised of individuals who were once civilians. With that in mind, it opens the door to the possibility that the capacity to do right or wrong may not be directly associated with their police powers, but instead with a character defect that lies dormant until unleashed by other dynamics. Though difficult to grasp, it could be that society will simply have to accept the reality that there are people, who work as police officers, dispatchers, prison guards, attorneys, judges, and in an assortment of other law enforcement–related professions, who are just as apt to, and entirely willing to, partake in illegal activity. If this is the case, with the exception of their possessing a gun, badge, and police power, they are no different from individuals who work in other professions. Yet, this is not to minimize what is obviously a fundamental difference, but to point out that unbridled access, far-reaching authority, and unique opportunities are, for some, tangibles to take advantage of and, for others, tools needed to perform their jobs effectively. In any case, if the tendency to commit crime is present, then there is also the opportunity to advance illegal schemes, and to participate in misconduct, brutality, and criminal acts with protections not available to the civilian population.

Considering the many possibilities, it prompts one to wonder: Is there a difference in how people regard, for instance, an executive who ignores company policy or, for personal gain, looks the other way when a client uses inferior materials to produce consumer goods; versus the police officers who take money to ignore a crime that has been committed? A quick evaluation of both scenarios calls to mind potential factors such as poor judgment, a propensity for inappropriate behavior, moral weaknesses, and an overall susceptibility of yielding to temptation. Yet, there is an obvious difference when a police officer—or, for that matter, any member of the law enforcement community—is the perpetrator. The clear distinction is that when a sworn officer solicits bribes, ignores wrongdoing by looking the other way, or participates in criminal activity for personal gain, it is not only irrefutably corrupt, but also a flagrant violation of their sworn oath, an obvious misuse of police powers, but an affront to society.

For this and other reasons, it is imperative that the process for evaluating and selecting police recruits and accepting other criminal justice system personnel includes a rigorous assessment designed to gauge their critical thinking and to determine if an inclination for criminal behavior is present. Failure to do so has the potential of creating catastrophic results. However, if discovered in time, ideally before police power is conferred upon the individual, many problems can be avoided. For example, in 2014, a small-town police officer on the job for less than one week was fired for several counts of misconduct and charged with an alleged burglary. According to a July 12, 2014, *Chicago Tribune* article, Richmond officer Ryszard Kopacz was arrested on "charges of official misconduct, burglary and possessing stolen guns."[2]

According to Chuck Klein, similar to General Douglas MacArthur's famous 1962 explanation of the obligation of soldiers—"Duty, honor, country"—law enforcement officers are governed by a slightly modified creed: "Integrity, courage, and allegiance." When discussing the role of police officers, Klein strongly differentiated the work of police officers from other professions, saying that "Police officers are in the business of honesty. This is their stock-in-trade, forte, signature, persona, identification and what differentiates them from other professions." According to Klein, "Temptations abound to subvert those of power to commit lapses in discretion for the gains of favor."[3] To Klein, the law enforcement officer ethic, or LEO, is thorough in its requirements that relate to ethical behaviors and moral values that are clearly defined as: no lying, cheating, stealing, excuses, or exceptions.

Adherence to the qualities defined for LEOs start with integrity, courage, and allegiance. The description of these crucial and highly regarded attributes directly contradicts the makings of a dirty cop. For instance, when considering integrity as an unbending observance to righteousness both in their professional and personal lives, whether on duty or off duty, obviously it is not something that one associates with a corrupt police officer.

At the core of the police officer's creed is an allegiance that is eloquently expressed as being, "Sworn to act with ethical integrity and courage; add now the requisite of loyalty to their profession, their fellow officers, all of the laws, court rulings and constitutional mandates."[4]

LEOs refer to courage as something done by police officers across the country day in, day out. When police officers put themselves in life-threatening situations, they do so because it is their sworn duty to protect their fellow citizens. We should be mindful that they are also under enormous pressure from a variety of organizations, and that it takes a tremendous amount of fortitude to remain steadfast in their treatment of criminal suspects, especially given the overwhelming burden of keeping the public safe, balanced against the scrutiny of law enforcement watchdogs such as the American Civil Liberties Union (ACLU) and others.

Some experts believe that routine assessments should be conducted throughout one's law enforcement career in order to ascertain sustained suitability. This is especially important as it relates to psychological fitness and preemptive intervention to preclude stressors from becoming factors that could potentially impact the officer's performance. That said, the ultimate objective is being able to, as often as possible, head off problems or weed out individuals inclined to partake in acts of police misconduct, misuse of authority, extortion, crimes of opportunity, susceptibility to the lure of bribes, and other criminal acts. In addition to being essential to the proficient operation of law enforcement agencies and insuring that personnel are functioning at an optimal level, doing so provides ongoing monitoring of the integrity of our criminal justice apparatus, by focusing on the individuals that we depend on and who are sworn to serve and protect the rest of us. Considering that they are the bedrock of what is central to maintaining public trust in the criminal justice system, doing anything less would be imprudent.

In the April 2013 edition of *The Police Chief: The Professional Voice of Law Enforcement*, there is what is as close to an unequivocal assertion as one can imagine as it relates to the importance of the dependability of psychological soundness within the ranks of law enforcement personnel: "[A]ssessing the psychological suitability of candidates for law enforcement positions is one of the essential functions of police psychology."[5] For example, some psychological service organizations that have the expertise in evaluating the fitness of individuals applying for law enforcement positions, especially in the pre-employment phase, encourage the use of controlled studies to aid in determining the most effective way to predict the performance of police officers. The intent is equivalent to an emotional vetting that is carried out during the pre-employment phase. It among other things is used to evaluate the recruit's ability to function under a variety of circumstances, including an assessment of tolerance under extreme conditions as well as one's ability to maintain honesty and to use good judgment, particularly when no one is looking.

Of course, there are indicators that warrant closer scrutiny and that are especially worrying, because they represent what could be a forewarning of future adverse behavior. In some instances, the troubling signs are evidenced in traits such as an aversion to hard work, the refusal to follow orders, a display of deviousness, and an overly aggressive temperament. Still, it is not irrefutable evidence that there is a looming problem that will escalate. It is important to remember that negative behaviors that are displayed by police recruits, and even veteran police officers, are sometimes anomalies that, if too heavily considered, could result in eliminating individuals who are not only fit for duty, but also prime candidates for a law enforcement career. Not only that, but it is a fine line wherein additional factors such as life experience, environment, and other contributing influences must be weighed. Without doing so, the door is opened to unfair treatment and exclusion of an individuals that could very well go on to serve the public in a long and stellar career in law enforcement.

As a case in point, in police departments across the country, there are veteran police officers who perform their jobs well, and many who have been repeatedly recognized for their dedication and bravery. There is absolutely no reason to question their loyalty and honesty as police officers, or to assume that they fit the profile of one day becoming a dirty police officer. However, because their behavior is sometimes perceived as being overzealous and over the top, many of them face intense scrutiny and are frequently cautioned by the police command. As a result, careers are affected, and their promotional potential is impeded.

The reality is that the stringent procedures intended to scrutinize recruits during the pre-employment process and to continue intermittingly throughout the career of police officers can be an arduous two-edged proposition that has been proven fallible time and again. On one hand, some reform-minded law-enforcement advocates suggest that any hint of flawed judgment or a penchant for misconduct should be enough to signal that the risk for an escalation of problems that could affect the individual's performance and critical thinking at a pivotal moment is rationale for exclusion. That said, licensed police psychologists having expertise in personnel screening as it relates to public safety, when assessing a prospective police recruit's emotional stability, personality traits, and history to determine suitability to serve as a police officer, are equipped with an extensive and, considered by many, extremely intrusive background check to aid in their assessment of the individual.

Of course, a comprehensive going-over of one's background is not foolproof, and in cases where an officer's conduct comes under scrutiny because of an allegation or finding of misconduct, depending on one's perspective, it is relatively easy to identify signs of potential trouble, or nothing at all to indicate adverse behavior. In fact, in some instances, the rigors of psychological testing have failed to discover major indicators related to ethical suitability, mental health, or personal problems. This, despite the fact that the preliminary screening and detailed background checks required by law enforcement is thought by some police personnel to be tantamount to the degradation of a strip search.

Experts generally agree that things like drug and alcohol abuse, domestic violence, and financial difficulties can be key indicators and are undesirable traits in prospective police recruits. However, this is by no means a guarantee that the person is guaranteed to become a corrupt cop. Even when utilizing an assortment of background checks, psychological examinations, and lie detector tests, there is no surefire method to determine the suitability of an individual to serve as a police officer, or to work in any capacity of our criminal justice system. Yes, there is the often-referred-to "red flag," but the only conclusive truth is that it depends entirely on the individual, their choices, and how they apply life experience to the situations that they encounter.

Sharon Hughes, founder and president of the Center for Changing Worldviews, while doing research, came across an article titled "The Perfect Cop"; its author is unknown. In this parody, the perfect cop is described from a variety of interesting perspectives.

To a Police Chief, the perfect cop is someone who looks sharp, works hard and doesn't expect overtime pay, makes good arrests without offending anyone, writes detailed reports and keeps a neat, readable activity log. He is also always available when extra help is needed, accepts work assignments willingly and comes up with fast, favorable results. In short, a perfect cop is someone who makes the Chief look good.

To a Prosecuting Attorney, a perfect cop is a meticulous investigator who gathers and documents evidence, obtains confessions to all crimes and outlines each case in order to make the prosecutor's job easy. He doesn't object when a case is plea bargained so the attorneys can go golfing on Friday afternoon, and doesn't mind if an offender gets probation or a suspended sentence because it is more convenient to make a deal than go to trial.

To a Defense Attorney, a perfect cop is a bungling idiot who makes mistakes and someone the defense attorney can manipulate and make angry in court, making the attorney look good in front of his client. A perfect cop is someone who will agree to any and all plea-bargaining proposed, and whom the defense attorney can call when he needs protection from his own client.

To the City Council, a perfect cop is someone who does his job well without making waves, who is grateful for a job that he willingly works nights, weekends and holidays. He never asks for more than the city is willing to pay, does an exemplary job without adequate equipment and tools. Best of all, he never writes tickets on any council member or their kid.

To the People of the Community, a perfect cop is polite, a friendly person who walks the beat and checks out strange noises and watches for strange people. He teaches kids right from wrong, talks to them about the evils of drug use—but doesn't mention Mom and Dad using alcohol. He will arrest drug dealers, but overlooks kids with a "little" pot.

To his Wife, a perfect cop never lets his job effect his emotions. He can spend hours dealing with drunks, domestics, drug users, injured or dead people, and then come home and be a loving, well-adjusted husband and father.[6]

The anonymous description of a perfect cop might strike a seasoned police officer as balderdash, and something that does not take into account the seamy world that police officers must contend with every day. They might also take exception with the exclusion of the role that politics plays in the responsibilities of a police officer, especially in an urban setting. However, there is also the reality for a police officer to embody every attribute described in "Perfect Cop," while at the same time being a dirty cop. Burge, Peterson, Dorner, and Valle all were at one time highly respected and decorated police officers who ultimately came to represent the most imperfect and reprehensible examples in the law enforcement community.

The personification of a dirty cop, or one whose misconduct infringes on an individual's constitutional rights, could bring both civil and criminal repercussions. It is not easy to substantiate allegations against police officers engaged in acts that deny or impede one's constitutional rights. However, within the last decade, things have started to change, and proving acts of harassment, excessive force, fabricating evidence, racial slurs, unjustified arrests, racial profiling, and other coercive acts have a better chance of being proven or disproven, mostly due to the proliferation of cell phones and other highly effective technology.

A watershed moment occurred on March 3, 1991, when after a high-speed chase, four Los Angeles police officers dragged a California black man named Rodney Glen King from the vehicle he was driving and brutally beat him. According to Biography.com, unbeknownst to LAPD police officers Laurence Powell, Timothy Wind, Theodore Briseno, and Stacey Koon, an amateur photojournalist named George Holliday was filming the entire assault against King. The nation watched the video in horror and disbelief. Suddenly, those who had refused to believe that LAPD officers would participate in such flagrant acts of misconduct and brutality were faced with the irrefutable proof of blatant excessive force. The overwhelming evidence of an assault with a deadly weapon and excessive force by the police officers resulted in a criminal indictment naming all four officers.

In the beginning, the officers were to be tried by a jury of their peers for their alleged crimes in the Los Angeles courts. However, citing probable bias, a change of venue was unanimously approved by the California Court of Appeals, and Judge Kamins, the original presiding judge, was removed from the case. Ultimately, the proceedings were moved to Simi Valley, a predominantly white suburb of Los Angeles. Moreover, and further inflaming racial tension, the jury was comprised of 10 white jurors, one Hispanic, and one Asian. This infuriated the black community, who speculated that the criminal justice system of Los Angeles County had rigged the proceedings, and in spite of the overpowering evidence against the officers, after a three-month-long trial, all four officers were acquitted of all charges.

The immediate response from the black community and advocates of fair treatment and justice was one of indignation. The fact that police brutality against King had been captured on camera yet regarded with insensitivity prompted an immediate and intense response. Many blacks who prior to the King incident had been extremely suspicious of the LAPD and the judicial process felt vindicated in their skepticism, and when the not guilty verdict was announced on April 29, 1992, they responded in anger. Within a matter of hours, their outrage turned into an explosion of rioting, looting, and utter chaos. To them, the not guilty verdict represented not only a miscarriage of justice, but also a total disregard for the treatment of blacks by the criminal justice system.

During the three days of rioting in South Central Los Angeles, more than 50 people were killed, 2,000 injured, and 9,500 people arrested for rioting, looting, and arson. Property damage estimates were as high as $1 billion. After days of nonstop rioting, in a public statement, King uttered his now-famous appeal: "People, I just want to say, can't we all get along? Can't we all get along?"[7]

Eventually, the U.S. Department of Justice filed civil rights charges against the police officers. In the end, two were found guilty, and two were acquitted of all charges. As for King, he would receive an award of $3.8 million in a civil trial for the injuries he sustained as a result of the severe beating. Years later, a reflective King said, "As far as having peace within myself, the one way I can do that is forgiving the people who have done wrong to me. It causes more stress to build up anger. Peace is more productive."[8]

King's expressed reconciliation of his personal mistreatment by LAPD officers does not resolve the perplexing dichotomy and broader problem that exists between whites and minorities as it relates to claims of police brutality and the contrasting perception of police officers. For far too many

urban blacks, cops of every ethnicity are assumed to be vicious, racist, and crooked until proven otherwise. It is obviously true that a combination of things contribute to the making of a dirty cop, and having said that, an increasing number of people believe that a growing number of police officers are as corrupt as, or worse than, the criminals who prey on the public. Some go as far as to suggest that not only are police corruption and dirty cops the norm, but that the problem is so out of control, and that police departments have given up their battle to get rid of them. Some attempt to corroborate these claims by citing incidents like the infamous LAPD Rampart Scandal.

THE RAMPART SCANDAL

According to a PBS *Frontline* report, the Rampart Scandal is said to be the most malicious case of law enforcement corruption in the history of the LAPD. The scandal and the allegations of a chain of police dishonesty throughout the LAPD resulted in the overturning of approximately 100 criminal convictions and settlements in the millions, with taxpayer dollars. The shameful details of the scandal began coming to light in March 1997, when an LAPD undercover officer, Frank Lyga, shot and mortally wounded Kevin Gaines, an off-duty LAPD officer, in what was believed to be a case of road rage. The shooting of Gaines, a black officer, by Lyga, a white officer set off a media frenzy that rocked the LAPD. Lyga claimed that he had shot Gaines in self-defense when Gaines threatened him with a gun. In a statement to *Frontline*, Lyga said, "In my training experience this guy had 'I'm a gang member' written all over him."[9] In the course of the investigation, it was alleged that Gaines had previously been involved in similar incidents of road rage and had wielded a gun. In addition, it was revealed that Gaines was connected to the rap-recording label Death Row Records, known for hiring off-duty police officers as security guards. After three separate LAPD investigations concluded that the shooting was not racially driven, Lyga was permitted to return to duty as a LAPD police officer.

Several months later, a Los Angeles branch of Bank of America was robbed of $722,000. From the start, the investigation focused on Errolyn Romero, an assistant bank manager. Not long after, Romero came clean, owning up to her role in the robbery and implicating her boyfriend, LAPD officer David Mack, as the architect of the crime. Mack and two other officers, including Mack's partner Rafael Perez—a member of the LAPD's Community Resources Against Street Hoodlums (CRASH), a select unit of officers responsible for combating gang-related crime—had gambled away thousands of dollars in Las Vegas just days after the robbery. Mack received 14 years in federal prison for his crime, and while serving his sentence, Mack fraternized with the Mob Piru Bloods, who had gang ties to Death Row Records.

In 1998, alleged gang member Ismael Jimenez was brought to the Rampart police station for questioning and, while handcuffed, was beaten by LAPD officer Brian Hewitt. Following an internal investigation, Hewitt was fired, and Jimenez was awarded $231,000 in a civil settlement with the city. Later that year, six pounds of cocaine went missing from the LAPD property room, and within a short time, LAPD officer Perez was under investigation.

Perez, who moved from Puerto Rico to the East Coast as a boy, was like many other young men who wanted to become a police officer. Perez told the *Los Angeles Times* that "[a]s far back as I can remember I knew I wanted to be a police officer."[10] In 1989, Perez's dream came true when he was sworn in as a member of the LAPD. During his time at the police academy, he was a squad leader and known as a good cop. Several years after joining the LAPD, Perez was assigned to an undercover narcotics squad known as a "buy team." It is during this time that he and Officer Mack became partners.

According to Perez, the turning point when he went from a good cop to a bad cop came in the mid-1990s. It was after joining the LAPD's Rampart antigang CRASH unit when Perez began stealing drug money. The slide into the abyss of criminal activity continued with Perez stealing cocaine and selling it for personal gain. Eventually, when confronted with a long prison sentence, he began to talk with prosecutors, implicating other LAPD police officers also assigned to the CRASH team.

According to a PBS *Frontline* report, when sentenced in 2000, Perez apologized, taking full responsibility for his illicit activities. Perez also spoke to the court about the manner in which police power acts as an intoxicant, saying that he was ultimately consumed by the us-against-them ethos of the overzealous cop. "We vaguely sensed we were doing the wrong things for the right reasons. Time and again, I stepped over that line. Once crossed, I hurdled over it again and again, landing with both feet sometimes on innocent persons. My job became an intoxicant that I lusted after," said Perez.[11]

In spite of the fact that Perez had failed five polygraphs and that he was despised by police officers, who considered him a thief, scam artist, and liar, a number of Perez's revelations about LAPD corruption and the police misconduct were corroborated. Moreover, Perez's testimony provided chilling insight regarding the controlling effect that police power has over some officers, and how in turn, they exert their authority over others. By connecting the allure of police power in terms of being an intoxicant, Perez's description was perceived as a succinct illustration of the realities that exist inside law enforcement agencies throughout the country. Perez's description of the fine line that police officers must walk not only was instrumental in the decision to terminate LAPD's CRASH program, but it also initiated an investigation by the LAPD that resulted in over 100 recommendations to improve practices related to police hiring, training, and supervisory oversight. Eventually, Perez's revelations caused the LAPD hierarchy to staff the gang taskforce with more experienced police officers.

PSYCHOLOGICAL SCREENING FOR POLICE OFFICERS

In a perfect world, the prerequisite psychological evaluation and battery of tests required for police candidates prior to taking a sworn oath and becoming police officers would weed out individuals who exhibit tendencies suggesting that, down the road, problems related to ethics would likely surface. While the rigorous pre-employment criterion is essential and tremendously helpful in evaluating and in some cases disqualifying prospective problem candidates, it is soundly agreed that it is not foolproof. Psychological and medical pre-employment assessments, which measure things like integrity, substance abuse, and a disabling mental condition that might impact judgment under extremely stressful conditions, are intended to evaluate the suitability of the prospective candidate, and do in fact achieve a measure of success.

According to *Police Chief: The Professional Voice of Law Enforcement*, as it relates to the question of suitability and the criterion used by law enforcement agencies to evaluate candidates, the screening processes are essential to all facets of the law enforcement community.

> Preemployment psychological screening can be used as part of the selection process for sworn officers and also for dispatchers, confidential records personnel, crime scene technicians, and evidence and property custodians. All of these employees in a law enforcement agency must be able to tolerate the stresses of working in a fast-paced environment, follow rules, use resources responsibly, behave in a trustworthy manner, use good judgment, and refrain from off-duty behavior that would reflect poorly on the department. Thus, although the preemployment psychological evaluation is a critical part of the selection process for weapon-carrying officers,

it also is a valuable screening tool for applicants to other job classifi-
cations in a law enforcement agency. In these screening assessments,
psychological suitability refers to both the absence of job-relevant
risk factors and the presence of job-critical personal and interper-
sonal qualities.

It is rare for even a poorly performing officer to be mentally ill.
Instead, applicants who are regarded as poorly suited for work in
law enforcement demonstrate a variety of counterproductive behaviors or characteristics including a lack of initiative, unwillingness to
follow rules, argumentativeness with their supervisors, untrustworthi-
ness, and over aggressiveness. Poor performers also may abuse alcohol
or drugs, both on and off the job. In fact, police managers have
observed that the majority of their departments' liability cases and
domestic abuse problems involve intoxicated off-duty officers. Job-
relevant risk factors considered by psychologists during the preem-
ployment assessment include mental or emotional conditions that
would reasonably be expected to interfere with safe and effective
job performance.[12]

Moreover, *Police Chief* points out that candidates who are seriously considered for positions as law enforcement officers, aside from clearing the
hurdles of psychological scrutiny, must also go through the invasive process of background investigations. It is an examination of their personal
history that generally includes information related to the applicant's edu-
cational history, employment history, compliance with laws and regula-
tions, recent illegal drug abuse, familial interactions, financial difficulties,
self-perceived weaknesses, reasons for wanting to work in law enforcement, and medical history that may have psychological relevance to their
employment as a police officer. For example, a medical history that is associated with psychiatric treatment, prescribed medications, alcohol abuse,
legal and illegal drug use, or a history of sexual misconduct, domestic violence, or suicidal ideas or attempts are relevant. Nonetheless, the psychological evaluation, drug screening, and complete pre-employment process
so crucial to the prospective law enforcement candidate hinges on the
psychological testing component, which does not, with 100 percent accu-
racy, determine the individual's suitability as a candidate for a career in law
enforcement.

Timothy Roufa, who has over a decade of experience as a police
academy instructor, provides unique insight into the significance of one's
pursuit of a career in law enforcement. Roufa's understanding of the
pressures that law enforcement personnel face is spot-on.

There are a lot of demands placed upon law enforcement, and a day in the life of a police officer can be emotionally, mentally and physically taxing. There will be days when you are forced to stand firm yet polite in the face of tremendous verbal abuse, and there will be times when you are exposed to horrific scenes. The fact of the matter is, not everyone is cut out for a career as a cop. While it takes all kinds of personalities to make up an effective police force, there are certain traits all officers should ideally share.

Conversely, there are also certain traits that are generally agreed to be undesirable in law enforcement officers. The psychological tests tend to focus on identifying those undesirable traits more than look for those desirable traits. It's important to remember that if your screening finds one or more of those traits, it's not a reflection on your value, your sanity or your personality; it's very narrowly focused toward your suitability to become a police officer.[13]

Roufa's expert opinion is in alignment with the reality of a police officer's daily routine much more than the previously mentioned description of the "Perfect Cop." However, getting to the root problem, or proven correlations that contribute to taking a previously good cop like Perez and others described in the Rampart Scandal, is difficult. The complexity of doing so is seen in the barrage of media coverage related to corruption within the ranks of the law enforcement community.

Former New York mayor Michael Bloomberg and NYPD chief of police Raymond Kelly on a regular basis had to defend the city's stop-and-frisk policy. Both have said that the highly controversial measure became necessary after 9/11. However, critics of the sanctioned procedure felt that the stop-and-frisk policy contributes to racism and increases the opportunity for police misconduct. Oppositionists to stop-and-frisk assert that giving police officers the power to, at a whim, stop and frisk the general public crosses the line. Not only that, but naysayers believe that stop-and-frisk laws are a factor in the escalation of crime committed by police officers because, according to them, the power to detain and frisk an individual at any time offers an opportunity for misconduct, under the guise of performing their sworn duty.

A 2012 article by Ross Tuttle and Erin Schneider of the *Nation* describes an incident recorded by a New York City teenager, "Alvin," on June 3, 2011, while being subjected to a stop-and-frisk by NYPD officers. The ability of the Harlem teenager to capture on audio the sequence of events related to the stop-and-frisk helped to bring public awareness to the contentious and divisive course of action decided on by the NYPD to control criminal activity. Alvin's concealed taping also facilitates exposing the public to how the NYPD's discriminatory policy, and the unethical behavior of some its police officers, contribute to the public's perception of the dirty cop.

Using his cell phone, the teenager recorded what occurred during a stop-and-frisk by three plainclothes NYPD officers. According to the *Nation* article, first of all there was no valid legal reason for the officers stopping the teenager, or to use racial slurs and threaten the teenager with bodily harm. In spite of the absence of reasonable cause to detain him this is how the incident is described, with the audio recording supporting the teenager's claims: "Early in the stop, one of the officers asks, 'You want me to smack you?' When Alvin asks why he is being threatened with arrest, the other officer responds, 'For being a fucking mutt.' Later in the stop, while holding Alvin's arm behind his back, the first officer says, 'Dude, I'm gonna break your fuckin' arm, then I'm gonna punch you in the fuckin' face.' "[14]

According to former NAACP president Ben Jealous, the outrageous behavior captured by Alvin's recording demonstrates how the abusive policies linked to programs like the NYPD stop-and-frisk program contribute to urban youths ambivalent and negative feelings toward the police. Donna Lieberman, executive director of the New York Civil Liberties Union, went further, saying that Alvin's audiotape is undisputable proof to the general public that "[t]hey are repeatedly subjected to abusive and disrespectful treatment at the hands of the NYPD. This explains why so many young people don't trust the police and won't help the police."[15]

In 2013, when Federal Judge Shira A. Scheindlin ruled New York's controversial "stop-and-frisk" unconstitutional, I used my weekly newspaper column to offer my viewpoint:

> From the beginning, New York City's Stop and Frisk law was on a slippery slope, and believed destined to result in charges of systemic racial profiling. Studies indicate that the New York City Police Department had used an unfair system of justice, with a particular biased toward black men. Not long ago a federal judge brought the controversial program to an abrupt halt.
>
> Federal Judge Shira A. Scheindlin, in her 195-page decision, concluded that black men had been disproportionately subjected to the Stop and Frisk program.
>
> It was disclosed that over a 10-year period, since the program began, more black men had been subjected to NYPD's crime-fighting deterrent than New York City's entire eight million-plus population.

The statistics tell the story of the individuals who put up with the city's crime-fighting program. A staggering 52 percent were black and 31 percent Hispanic.

What Scheindlin's lengthy decision said about the NYPD's Stop and Frisk law is what those affected had already figured out, that not only is the program a violation of the Fourth Amendment, but also a clear example of police powers on steroids.

Scheindlin ruled that the NYPD had over time developed what she referred to as a "policy of indirect racial profiling" as it increased the number of stops in minority communities. That has led to officers' routinely stopping "blacks and Hispanics who would not have been stopped if they were white."

In strong and to the point language, Scheindlin talked about the "human toll of unconstitutional stops," describing every instance of Stop and Frisk as "a demeaning and humiliating experience . . ." noting that "no one should live in fear of being stopped whenever he leaves his home to go about the activities of daily life."

Profiling is a polarizing issue that presents a dichotomy for urban America. This is especially true in minority communities, where demands that law enforcement do more to stop the senseless violence grows louder. Therefore, taking a position against Stop and Frisk can be viewed as a contradiction of what law enforcement agencies are tasked with doing in order to make communities safer.

A livid NYPD Chief of Police Ray Kelly responded to the Scheindlin's order by saying that minority communities will be the losers. Kelly said on "Meet the Press" that "If Stop and Frisk were abandoned, no question about it—violent crime will go up."

Anyone who reads my column knows that when it comes to guns and gang violence, I am consistently on the side of doing whatever is necessary to protect our children, and the innocent. In communities where gang violence puts lives at risk, law enforcement must have the ability to be aggressive, and to take a stand. On the other hand, I believe that Scheindlin's order was necessary, and from my point of view, her recommendation to outfit police officers with small cameras to record Stop and Frisk incidents seems to be a reasonable first step toward a more fair and effective program.

In order to get the perspective of a local law enforcement leader, I contacted Aurora Police Chief Greg Thomas, who heads a police department whose success in battling violence and gangs is nationally known. Thomas explained how in the 1968 landmark "Terry v. Ohio" case, the United States Supreme Court ruling established that

Stop and Frisk does not violate the Fourth Amendment, thereby allowing law enforcement to use the technique in its crime-fighting arsenal.

Thomas went on to explain that the ruling specifies that there must be a reasonable suspicion that the person has committed, is committing, or is about to commit a crime. In order to frisk, the officer must believe that there's a probability that the individual is armed and dangerous. Thomas stressed that just because an individual is stopped does not automatically mean that they will be subjected to a frisk.

"Stop and Frisk is a controversial policing procedure. However, if used properly, trained officers are able to strike the proper and intended balance between the freedoms guaranteed by the Fourth Amendment and law enforcement's responsibilities to serve and protect," Thomas said.

Now, that's as sensible an explanation of the police procedure as I have heard.

At the center of the Stop and Frisk scrutiny is the killing of 17-year-old Trayvon Martin. Across the country, Martin's killing is a symbol in the black community of racial profiling that has infiltrated the general population. The phenomenon is epitomized by individuals, who are not sworn police officers, yet who act as if they have the authority to exercise police powers.

Profiling is a word that was routinely used as the political machines geared-up for the 2014 mid-term elections, and kickoff the 2016 presidential race.

Case in point, politicians will seek out other instances of profiling that exists beyond the racial profiling that law enforcement is accused of perpetrating. They might, for example, focus on the stigma, psychological impact and unfair treatment alleged by members of the LGBT community, who have ample evidence that they are routinely profiled on the basis of their gender.

To be sure, profiling is a polarizing issue, and one that I'll have more to say about.[16]

For some onlookers, the question quickly becomes one that relates to whether police officers like those who participated in the sort of behavior perpetrated by the Rampart NYPD police officers, and those that are rarely held accountable for their actions, is a probable precursor of even more sinister acts of criminality?

It is more often the case that potentially dirty cops, or those who have already crossed the line, manage to keep their undesirable qualities under the radar for extended periods of time. In many cases they never answer for their indiscretions, misconduct, and corrupt acts. Occasionally, their misdeeds come to light as a result of conspiratorial activities, internal investigations, confidential sources, anonymous tips, and serendipity. However, more often, many are able to keep their misdeeds and undesirable behavior concealed, sometimes for their entire career.

NOTES

1. Frank Hague, quoted in Anthony Olszewski, "Frank Hague, Mayor of Jersey City, 1917–1947," http://www.cityofjerseycity.org/hague/ (accessed April 29, 2013).

2. Dan Hinkel, *Chicago Tribune*, July 12, 2014.

3. Chuck Klein, "Police Ethics: The Creed," LawOfficer.com, October 23, 2012, http://www.lawofficer.com/article/leadership/police-ethics-creed (accessed May 28, 2013).

4. Ibid.

5. Yossef S. Ben-Porath, James M. Fico, Neil S. Hibler, Robin Inwald, Joelle Krumi, and Michael R. Roberts, "Assessing the Psychological Suitability of Candidates for Law Enforcement Positions," *Police Chief: The Professional Voice of Law Enforcement*, April 2013, http://www.policechiefmagazine.org/magazine/index.cfm?fuseaction=display&article_id=2448&issue_id=82011 (accessed April 29, 2013).

6. Sharon Hughes, "Crooked and Straight Cops," *RenewAmerica*, February 16, 2014, http://www.renewamerica.com/columns/hughes/040216 (accessed April 30, 2013).

7. "Rodney King Biography," Biography.com, http://www.biography.com/people/rodney-king-9542141 (accessed May 2, 2013).

8. Ibid.

9. "Rampart Scandal Timeline," *Frontline*, http://www.pbs.org/wgbh/pages/frontline/shows/lapd/scandal/cron.html (accessed May 9, 2013).

10. Rick Young, "Rafael Perez: In the Eye of the Storm," *Frontline*, http://www.pbs.org/wgbh/pages/frontline/shows/lapd/scandal/eyeofstorm.html (accessed May 16, 2013).

11. Ibid.

12. Ben-Porath et al., "Assessing the Psychological Suitability of Candidates for Law Enforcement Positions."

13. Timothy Roufa, "Psychological Exams and Screening for Police Officers," http://criminologycareers.about.com/od/Job_Market/a/Psychological-Screening-For-Police-Officers.htm (accessed May 27, 2013).

14. Ross Tuttle and Erin Schneider, "Stopped-and-Frisked for Being a F**king Mutt," *Nation*, October 8, 2012, http://www.thenation.com/article/170413/stopped-and-frisked-being-fking-mutt-video#ixzz2UDI3VPBy (accessed May 29, 2013).

15. Ibid.

16. Anthony Stanford, *Beacon-News*, August 24, 2013, http://posttrib .chicagotribune.com/search/22134408-418/striking-the-balance-between -security-individual-rights.html#.VImlRKYqlMw (accessed October 1, 2013).

5

❖

Mounting Excessive Force in Reaction to Political Pressure

"People sleep peaceably in their beds at night only because rough men stand ready to do violence on their behalf."[1]

The preservation of law and order—or, possibly more importantly, the appearance of it—is extremely important to the American people's psyche. As has been noted, law enforcement officials are prepared to go to extremes to maintain a compliant law-abiding society, or at the very least, a believable likeness of one that eases the minds of the people. The benefit of doing so is significant in a number of ways, some that are directly related to maintaining law and order, and others that are tangentially associated with the police officer's oath to serve and protect. However, the truth is that in both instances, politics rules the day. The inference of a crime-ridden culture in contemporary society adversely affects every segment of our social order. The public's confidence that law enforcement agencies have crime under control, and are removing from society those who would commit crimes and do bodily harm to others, not only brings comfort, but also supports the tenets of our democracy. Yet, the reality is that it is a political imperative to promote, regardless of its veracity, the notion of public safety.

If perception is reality, then citizens view their security much differently today from how they did several decades ago. The people that shape our opinion concerning law and order have the increasingly difficult task of convincing us that our safety is their primary concern and, equally tough, that they are actually maintaining it. Clearly, we are vulnerable, and our susceptibility is illustrated in a number of ways—for instance, the ongoing menace posed by foreign or domestic acts of terrorism against the homeland. After 9/11, this particular threat prompted a new phrase in the American lexicon— "remain vigilant"—of which we are constantly reminded. So, when considering this warning, the truth is that it is our individual vigilance more than a catchy phrase, but key to our security. As a result of continued terrorist threats, Americans have had to modify their behavior and to surrender some of the freedoms once taken for granted.

Easy access to guns, drugs, the random killing of innocent people, high-tech crimes such as identity theft, and threats against water treatment and utilities systems are all factors that are wearing thin the public's confidence in our law enforcement organizations. Societal factors, which include high unemployment, poverty, and corporate wrongdoing, add to soaring crime rates, as do offenses like child pornography and the use of social media to perpetrate inventive scams targeting unsuspecting victims and the elderly. Last, but certainly not least, are hate crimes and a brand of vigilante justice that is perpetrated by civilians who carry out criminal acts against others. This variety of street justice is thought by some to be buttressed by the crimes perpetrated by police officers that, through their misdeeds and acts of brutality, send a contradictory message to some in the civilian population that taking matters into their own hands is acceptable. Moreover, the inconsistency exposes the entire criminal justice system to claims of duplicity and contributes to the erosion of our values.

In large American cities like New York, Chicago, Los Angeles, Atlanta, and Philadelphia, police hierarchies struggle with ways to maintain public safety and the confidence of the general public. An integral part of law enforcement training is to give the impression that even when faced with facts in direct contradiction, things are under control. In Chicago, where urban violence and the killing of innocent children is frequently reported by the national media and amplified with the gruesome and tragic details of their untimely deaths, a pall hangs over the communities where the violence has, so far, been unabated. Violent death in urban America is so common that it is nonchalantly recorded and often presented as cold matter-of-fact statistics, at the ready, for use by politicians, crime-fighting activists, and the media.

Garry McCarthy, the superintendent of the Chicago Police Department (CPD), came under fire for the city's horrendous 2012 surge of violence

and soaring murder rate. McCarthy has on a number of occasions implemented pioneering strategies that are aimed at bringing down the crime
rate and relieving the fears of Chicagoans, some of whom reside in neighborhoods that resemble war zones. However, the reality is that in some
urban communities, gang violence, shootings, and random killings are
considered a way of life. Some believe that it will take the implementation
of a variety of policing strategies, some of them controversial, to interrupt
the violence.

According to a *Chicago Magazine* article:

Fair or not, much of that responsibility falls on the superintendent of
the Chicago Police Department, a position that is so intense, political, and high-profile that former chiefs say they never expected to
hold on to the job for more than a few years. Enter Garry Francis
McCarthy, a hard-charging vet of police departments in New York
City and Newark, New Jersey. [Mayor Rahm] Emanuel brought him
to Chicago in May 2011 on a promise to address the city's gang problem, make the CPD run more efficiently, and rebuild officer morale.

But two months after McCarthy arrived, the murder toll—the stat
by which police superintendents are most judged—began to inch
upward. And after a brief winter respite, violence surged in March
of this year. Through June 17, police reported 240 homicides, a
38 percent increase over the same period in 2011. The situation is
particularly worrisome in light of statistics that show the number of
murders and shootings starting to level off before McCarthy and
Emanuel took over.

Of course, many factors contribute to an uptick in urban violence.
But the current crime wave raises questions about the decisions made
by McCarthy—an outsider who arrived in Chicago armed with a
playbook of policing strategies he learned on the East Coast—and
the man who has been his primary supporter, Mayor Emanuel. Why
don't the crime-fighting strategies that worked so effectively in
New York and Newark seem to be working here? And if they aren't
working, why isn't McCarthy changing them? If the violence continues at the same troubling rate, the city will surely demand answers,
and McCarthy, who was once compared to George Washington,
John Wayne, and Braveheart, could receive a much less flattering
title: ex-superintendent.[2]

However, it is fair to say that by 2013, McCarthy was able to
report some, though minimal, success in reducing violent crime in

several communities. Although he attributed the accomplishment to newly implemented policing tactics, surely he knows that the complexity of the violence problem in Chicago's inner city will take years and a deployment of radical approaches to slow. McCarthy—for that matter, any police superintendent of a large metropolitan police force—understands that satisfying the public is directly connected to the political power structure, and that the elected official has a personal stake in a superintendent's success or failure.

It may not be politically prudent to declare it so, but politics drives law enforcement efforts, and as Chicago's top cop, McCarthy must contend with what other high-ranking law enforcement officials throughout urban America must deal with on a regular basis. Many are, in my mind, controlled by the volatility of the political landscape and motivated by the body politic. The law enforcement community hierarchy especially understands that the success of the strategies that are employed to help control inner-city crimes such as murder, rape, and robberies are inextricably tethered to politics, ideologies, and power. A vote of confidence from powerful elected officials equates to an approval of the individual's ability to maintain control, arguably the essential factor used to gauge one's staying power. It is known throughout the law enforcement chain of command that more than anything else, convincing the public that crime is under control directly affects a law enforcement professional's chance to rise through the ranks of the high police command, as well as to enjoy longevity.

This is no less true for subordinate police officers who aspire to leadership positions. In the case of police officers who are newer to the profession, it is generally accomplished through the appeasement of their superiors, and by demonstrating through verifiable statistics a reduction in crime within their area. For example, taking violent offenders, gangbangers, rapists, drug dealers, and others prone to acts of criminality off the street, and thereby increasing a sense of security in violence-ravaged communities, is one way for a rank-and-file police officer to increase visibility, commendation, and opportunities for promotion.

However, McCarthy's situation is perhaps more what any other police superintendent in the country must deal with. Indeed, because of its very high profile and political nature, and the obvious professional risks to one's career, others might shy away from a position so greatly influenced by politics. In McCarthy's case, it is not only local politics, but on a grander and national scale. This is because as superintendent of police in the city that the president of the United States calls home, McCarthy's successes, failures, and strategies are constantly under intense scrutiny. Moreover, the former chief of staff to President Barack Obama, Rahm Emanuel, serves as mayor of Chicago, something that undoubtedly ratchets up the pressure and keeps Chicago's superintendent of police in the national spotlight.

The reality is that this scenario is true not only as it relates to the burden placed on McCarthy to offer proof that crime is being reduced under his command, but also in demonstrating that the policing methods implemented reflect a sustainable decline in the city's crime rate overall. Politicians are more likely to offer their support if they are satisfied that McCarthy's actions and progress are not merely a flash in the pan, but tangible and maintainable strategies to slow down the crime rate.

An illustration of the role that politics plays in policing tactics in urban communities, and of how the nation perceives violence in Chicago, was seen in 2013, when 15-year-old prep-school student Hadiya Pendleton was gunned down. The senseless shooting death of the teenager brought international media coverage focusing on Chicago's gang, gun, and violence epidemic. Fair or not, also on the firing line, some say, was McCarthy's job. The teenager's death is thought, by many, to be stark evidence of a monumental failure by the second-largest police force in the United States, some 13,400 police officers under McCarthy's command, to protect the 2,836,658 residents of Chicago.

As if the battle to control crime in inner-city neighborhoods is not enough, there is a relatively new criminal element that police commands are forced to contend with. Known as flash mobs, the advent of this high-tech crime is comprised of individuals whose ability to create instant havoc and to stretch police resources to the limit is perpetrated using advances in technology. Forming quickly, flash mobs are usually organized utilizing a variety of social media sites. There are those who utilize the technological know-how to garner attention to their artistic expression, and others to organize civilian protests. However, some use it to spur acts of criminality, such as unlawful assembly, looting, and mob action. Because of the spontaneous development, the flash mobs are difficult for police to control. Moreover, the ability of participants to rapidly disperse makes it difficult to identify the culprits. The chaotic situations produced by criminal flash mobs, and the public demand that police do something to stop them, has led to claims of excessive force and police brutality.

Emanating from political pressure, Illinois lawmakers are combating the phenomenon with a bill intended to crackdown on flash mob participants who incite violence and criminal behavior. Illinois representative Christian Mitchell (D-Chicago) sponsors a bill that would give judges the authority to apply prison sentences ranging from three to six years on individuals who are found guilty of using electronic communication to initiate mob violence. Mitchell said that "[t]his gives our law enforcement the ability to keep up with the changing times."[3] For some time now, the NYPD has been using police officers to monitor social media sites and to learn about gang and criminal activity while still in the planning stages. Some say that it is akin to the preemptive surveillance techniques utilized by the Central Intelligence Agency (CIA). According to *Chicago Tribune* columnist John Kass, "And now the Chicago Police Department—like its colleagues in New York—has detailed officers to watch gangsters get together and boast about who got capped, who fell and who should die."[4]

There is little doubt that the political quandary that confronts McCarthy in Chicago is being repeated, though much less publicly, throughout police departments across the country. In addition, it is reasonable to conclude that the allegations related to excessive force and police brutality are in some instances connected to the frustration associated with the inability to implement law enforcement strategies that better control and significantly reduce inner-city crime rates that are acceptable to the public, and that meet the ever-increasing demands of elected officials and would-be politicians.

In order to do so, police departments are utilizing innovative methods to deter gang violence. For example, the CPD works with a controversial organization called "CeaseFire," founded by epidemiologist Dr. Gary Slutkin. The organization is comprised of mostly ex-offenders whose role is to interrupt gang and gun violence. CeaseFire achieved international recognition in 2011 when one of its pioneering members, former CeaseFire director Tio Hardiman, came up with the idea of using ex-convicts as mediators to work in some of Chicago's toughest neighborhoods. Hardiman believed that interfering in planned and potential violence at an early stage would offer hope and results. A documentary about Operation CeaseFire, titled "The Interrupters," received critical acclaim and was the recipient of the 2011 Spirit Award.

However, in a city where the homicide rate exceeded 500 people for the second time in a decade, the relationship between CeaseFire and the CPD has not always been stress-free. The reason for this is that some of the former gang members don't trust police officers, and police officers don't trust and are reluctant to work with former gang members. In fact, some former gang members view the CPD's tactics as oppressive and draw on their personal encounters with police officers to exemplify the harassment and brutality that others find themselves up against. This allegation not only plagues the relationship, but can also diminish the success of the program. There is no doubt that the ongoing clash impedes the common goal shared by CeaseFire and CPD, which is to slow the rate of violence in Chicago.

Angalia Bianca, a CeaseFire Illinois supervisor, is a former heroin addict and gang member. She has been arrested over 120 times, and at various times has served more than 12 years in prison. Not one to hold her tongue, Bianca candidly talked about the sometimes-strained relationship that CeaseFire Illinois workers have with some Chicago police officers:

> Sometimes police will say to me "You guys are all felons!" their mindset is that we can't be rehabilitated, work a legal job and contribute in a meaningful way to society. My answer to that is "I once was a complete strain on the Illinois tax base including the 25 thousand dollars a year expense to house me in a prison, not to mention public aid, food stamps, free health care, court costs, and the affect of my crimes on humankind. Today, I am a law abiding productive citizen who is dedicated to the work I do. I pay taxes, vote and I am considered by many as a responsible, reliable and trustworthy community leader." My question to the skeptical police officer is, "What would you have me do today?" Police officers usually reply, "Well now that you put it that way!"[5]

Bianca asserts that the problem seems to stem from the fact that some police officers do not appreciate, and are opposed to, CeaseFire employees' exemption from being required to share the information that they become privy to as a result of their work and relationship with gang members while working in some of the city's toughest neighborhoods. However, Bianca argues, the police officers don't seem to understand that doing so would put CeaseFire workers in danger and render them ineffective in mediating conflicts, for the simple reason that gang members would no longer trust them. According to Bianca, the main reason that CeaseFire is effective in preventing violence is the trust that the organization has forged by working with active gang members and demonstrating to them that there are better choices to consider before crossing the line into violence, shootings, and murder. Bianca is firm in her unequivocal support and respect for the CPD and the job that cops are sworn to do. However, while she quickly concedes that their approaches are obviously different, that does not necessarily mean that they can't find common ground and continue to strive toward positive change.

Continuing, Bianca says that sometimes police see CeaseFire employees in a target area with high-risk gang members, and because the cops really don't understand, or agree, with the role and methodology utilized to reduce violence, they sometimes misinterpret what is often an attempt to engage gang members in an open and frank dialogue. Bianca's point is that some police officers view it as fraternization with the criminal element. In spite of the fact that police officers know how the CeaseFire model operates, it continues to cause tension.

For instance, Bianca says that there have been a number of occasions when police have ordered CeaseFire staff off the streets where they are contracted to work. When this occurs, and CeaseFire workers are forced to explain that they are paid by the state to work in high-risk target areas, some police officers become infuriated. Bianca explained the organization's core belief, saying, "CeaseFire is committed to improving the rapport with the CPD because at the end of the day we are working toward achieving this, and to do so, it is necessary to understand and to respect each other's roles."[6]

Mounting political pressure on police departments across the country to control crime is thought to contribute to a spike in allegations of police brutality, excessive force, and coerced criminal confessions. In a shocking statement, Princeton University's Dr. Cornel West declared that in America, the police shoot a black person every 28 hours. Appearing on the *Real Time with Bill Maher* television show in July 2013, Dr. West proclaimed, "The criminal justice system itself is criminal." Dr. West's comments are echoed in an article written by Adam Hudson, appearing in Occupy.com, in which he says, "Police officers, security guards, or self-appointed vigilantes extrajudicially killed at least 313 African-Americans in 2012, according to a recent study. This means a black person was killed by a security officer every 28 hours."[7]

The information is based on a report titled Operation Ghetto Storm, conducted by the antiracist activist organization the Malcolm X Grassroots Movement. The report indicated that "In July 2012, in the tradition of 'On Lynching' by Ida B. Wells-Burnet and 'We Charge Genocide' by William L. Patterson, the Malcolm X Grassroots Movement released a report that exposed the fact that in the first six months of the year a Black man, woman, or child was summarily executed by the police, and a smaller number of security guards and self-appointed vigilantes, [e]very 36 hours!"[8]

If it turns out that these numbers are accurate, the report goes a long way toward putting in the simplest form a reason for the prevalent distrust held by some in the black community toward the American justice system. The sentiment especially targets police officers who patrol inner-city streets, licensed security guards, and individuals who, more and more, believe themselves justified in taking matters into their own hands.

Moreover, reports like the one offered by the Malcolm X Grassroots Movement have more than a ring of truth, especially as it relates to cities such as Chicago, where there is a prevailing belief that political pressure and selfish ambitions were predominant factors in the reign of terror led by former Chicago police commander Burge and his infamous Midnight Crew. This variety of proven systemic police misconduct threatens the individual and collective trust that people have in the criminal justice system. There is no way to dodge the tangible proof of misconduct by some Chicago cops that was so obvious that it prompted two aldermen to promote the payment of $20 million to Burge victims who had not been compensated for the torture they sustained under his command. According to the *Chicago Tribune*, Aldermen Howard Brookins and Joe Moreno proposed that the money be used to help torture victims who were not compensated through the courts. Brookins said that, "(Police) credibility has suffered, and therefore the ability to fight crime in our communities has also suffered based on this . . . The city has lost millions of dollars. It is time to get this era behind us."[9]

Chicago crime statistics for the first three months of 2012 revealed a 60 percent increase in violent crime over the previous year. Therefore, one might assume that the surge in acts of violence reflects a corresponding increase in allegations of police brutality. Some law enforcement officials readily blame the upsurge of inner-city violence on gangs and warm weather. However, in recent years, criminologists have had a more difficult time explaining rising crime rates during the winter months. In some cases, homicides and shootings do not seem to be affected by the weather. According to the *Chicago Tribune*, James Fox, a professor of criminology, law, and public policy at Northeastern University in Boston, supports the contention that warmer weather plays a part in increasing violence. Fox emphasizes that "[i]n better weather, people are outside more, interacting more with neighbors, acquaintance even strangers, and there's greater opportunity for conflict than when it's cold and windy."[10] The assertion that warmer temperatures coincide with violent behavior was discussed in a July 2012 CBS report that focused on a Chicago heat wave, during which 20 people were shot and three killed over a three-day period.

According to Craig Anderson a University of Iowa professor's 2001 paper titled "Heat and Violence," in the United States, there are 2.6 percent more murders and assaults in the summer versus the winter. Anderson asserts that "hot summers produce a bigger increase in violence than cooler summers."[11] Former New York police officer Eugene O'Donnell, when talking about his days as a beat officer, put his folksy spin on the weather and crime correlation: "Jack Frost is the best policeman."[12]

A 2010 study spanning the years 1999–2004, focusing on the city of Cleveland and published in *Weather, Climate and Society*, supports the warmer-weather crime hypothesis. The study suggests a relationship between warmer weather and an increase in violent criminal acts, most notably domestic violence and assaults that did not involve the use of weapons and ended without serious injury. According to Dr. Scott Sheridan, coauthor of the Cleveland study, "Some of the reason is increase in aggressive behavior, but a lot of it has to do with more people interacting with each other when the weather is warmer."[13] Chicago CeaseFire data analyst Charlie Ransford, in the *Huffington Post*, also argued that warmer temperatures constantly have an effect on violence: "Shootings go way down in winter . . . There are half or less than half [the number of shootings] than there are in the summertime. Weather does make a difference. [With a] warmer Spring, its natural to think there will be an increase in homicides and shootings."[14] Chicago's former top-cop Jody Weis offered his take on warm weather and increasing crime theory: "We will never, never use warm weather as an excuse for an increase in violence . . . It is a factor . . . not an excuse."[15]

The warmer weather, violent crime theory is considered dubious by some, yet clear-cut to others, and could boil down to simple logic that during the warmer months, when more people interact, there is more crime than when inclement weather keeps people indoors. However, if the relationship between warmer weather and crime is factual, as some law enforcement experts believe it is, and crime actually rises when the weather is warmer, then it would seem reasonable to conclude that a rise in the number of people who allege police brutality also occurs as the mercury rises.

The entire climatic hypothesis is challenged by egregious incidents like the one occurring in Chicago during the winter of 2007, when a 265-pound Chicago cop, Anthony Abbate, viciously beat Karolina Obrycka, a 115-pound female bartender, because she refused to continue serving him alcohol. The Abbate civil case not only challenges the warm-weather theory, but Obrycka's attorneys were able to prove Abbate guilty of the brutal beating that was captured on videotape, as well as the fact that the Chicago Police Department's hierarchy had been complicit in shielding the ex-cop from the charges. Therefore, added to the question of weather and crime is whether or not it affects those who are sworn to serve and protect.

According to a local news report, "The jury, which consisted of three men and eight women, agreed. They accepted the argument that Abbate conspired with other officers to minimize the case against him, and that higher ups sought to soft-pedal the case so as not to damage the department's reputation." And, "The jury found Abbate's status as a cop afforded him a certain level of protection—not just from the rank and file—but also police brass."[16] In a subsequent civil proceeding, the victim was eventually awarded an $850,000 settlement.

DEPARTMENT OF JUSTICE INVESTIGATIONS

What is fairly certain is that reports of escalating systemic police brutality and misconduct throughout the country have resulted in a sharp increase in the number of investigations conducted by the Department of Justice (DOJ). Scores of criminal allegations against individual police officers and entire police departments are currently underway at the federal level. Furthermore, there appears to be absolutely no correlation to warmer weather.

There is, for example, the sensational 2005 case against five New Orleans police officers, Sergeants Kenneth Bowen, Robert Gisevius and Arthur Kaufman, and officers Anthony Villavaso and Robert Faulcon. In this instance, it seems that perilous weather conditions, racial bias, excessive force, conspiracy, improper prosecutorial interference, and politics culminated in a situation that, over several years, shook the New Orleans Police Department (NOPD) to its core. The officers, facing sentences ranging from 120 years to life in prison, were charged in what is commonly referred to as the "Danziger Trial," and it was immediately apparent that the case was tinged by elements that would affect the wider New Orleans community and potentially stain the reputation of the entire NOPD. However, at the time, it was difficult to fathom that innuendo, and other factors related to the case, would reach the highest levels of the federal government.

What is alleged to have happened in the aftermath of Hurricane Katrina, known to many as the "perfect storm," is perceived as a flagrant example of excessive force, brutality, and a conspiracy against the people of New Orleans. According to the *New Orleans Tribune*, after NOPD officers killed two unarmed individuals and wounded four others on the Danziger Bridge, Lieutenant Michael Lohman reportedly told other police officers that, "We can't have this look like a massacre."[17]

Some NOPD officers cooperated with the government with the hope of receiving lighter sentences. For his part, Lohman described a situation wherein a conspiracy to conceal what occurred in the wake of Hurricane Katrina began immediately following the shooting and continued for four years. According to original witness reports, NOPD officers came looking for trouble and initiated it when Officer Ignatius Hills, a black police officer, fired at an unarmed 14-year-old named Leonard Bartholomew.

Another NOPD police officer reported Officer Hills to have said, "I just tried to pop that little (N-Word)."[18]

In late 2013, U.S. district judge Kurt Engelhardt ordered a new case for the convicted NOPD officers who were charged with federal civil rights violations. Judge Engelhardt cited DOJ activities associated with the investigation of the officers as being, "highly unusual, extensive and truly bizarre."[19] There is more to come related to the Danziger Bridge incident and other DOJ investigations.

VIGILANTE JUSTICE

Shocked, saddened, outraged, and disappointed are words used to describe the acquittal of George Zimmerman in the death of teenager Trayvon Martin. In what turned into one of the most racially sensitive cases in recent years, Zimmerman, a neighborhood watch volunteer, shot and killed the 17-year-old Martin in Sanford, Florida, on February 26, 2012, as the young man walked home from a local store. The details of the case captured the attention of the American public and became one of the most racially divisive issues since 1991, when the brutal beating by Los Angeles police officers of African American Rodney King was videotaped. Many believe that Zimmerman's killing of Martin suggests a troubling scenario wherein the use of excessive force and police brutality that is frequently alleged by blacks and minorities has spread to the civilian population, and to people who serve in official and nonofficial roles related to security and neighborhood watch groups.

Before continuing, it is important to note that I share the perspective of those who believe that the Zimmerman trial was presided over by a judge who was fair and impartial, and that the six-woman jury that rendered the "not guilty" verdict did so based on the evidence that was made available to them during the trial, and the instructions provided to them at the outset of the trial. Numerous legal experts believe that the jury understood the significance of the case, and that they participated in serious deliberations before delivering a unanimous verdict acquitting Zimmerman. Moreover, many believe that the acquittal, based on the court's instructions and Florida's now infamous "Stand Your Ground" law, left them no other choice. Of course, the division related to the verdict was predictable, and in fact, had Zimmerman been found guilty, right-wing radical groups would have viewed such a verdict as unjust.

Having said that, I stand with those who believe the problem lies within our criminal justice system and that when it comes to the treatment of accused blacks, other minorities, and the economically disadvantaged, the American criminal justice system is demonstrably biased. In a column written prior to the Zimmerman verdict being announced, I contended:

> Whatever happened between Martin and Zimmerman is symbolic of our colossal failure to address the race problem and to narrow the breach. I have to tell you that after the verdict was announced, and I was able to fully comprehend what it represents, that as an African American father of three children, and a grandfather, the consequence of the Zimmerman acquittal is in my opinion a stain on our judicial system.
>
> From my point of view and that of parents raising children of color Zimmerman's acquittal represents an, in your face, example of the vulnerability and inequality that minorities are susceptible to when they come face to face with the American criminal justice system. It also implies that the excessive force and political speak related to controlling crime in America, has made its way into the mainstream, and that some individuals, because of reports of widespread police brutality, view police brutality and vigilante justice as acceptable behavior. As Americans we are grateful that we live in a nation of laws, but many people are unfairly treated by virtue of the manner in which some laws are administered, especially as it relates to minorities and the poor.
>
> This is most likely what President Obama was alluding to in March 2012 when he talked about the killing of Martin saying, "If I had a son, he'd look like Trayvon. . ." "I think Trayvon's parents are right to expect that all of us as Americans are going to take this with the seriousness it deserves, and we are going to get to the bottom of exactly what happened."[20]

However, the reality is that the trial, and certainly Zimmerman's acquittal, did not get to the bottom of what actually occurred in Sanford on that February night in 2012. In a trial based mostly on conjecture, the only thing proven by the prosecution and defense was that neither could convince a jury of exactly what occurred. Still, clearing Zimmerman of all charges in the killing of Martin has become the catalyst, and a call to action for the American people to stand against individuals and law enforcement strategies that predispose a segment of society to racial profiling, prejudicial laws, and police brutality. It seems unlikely that the DOJ will launch a civil rights investigation into the Zimmerman case. In fact, some argue that further investigation is not warranted. However, what is certain is that Americans remain deeply divided over the verdict, and there is a lingering dissatisfaction among blacks that the decision to totally exonerate Zimmerman was another indication of the inherent bias of our criminal justice system.

The killing of Martin created another one of those seminal moments in contemporary race matters. If nothing else, contentious issues like the Zimmerman trial tend to clarify the divide between the black and white viewpoints, especially as it relates to perceived injustices within the criminal justice system. Moreover, these pivotal incidents can bring about significant fear and frustration to the parents of minority children. Given the realities of contemporary society and limited options available to them to keep their children safe, parents must, from the time that children are able to understand, teach them the importance of demeanor, the use of common sense, and methods of diffusing potentially dangerous situations.

For instance, returning to the effect of politics on crime fighting, the NYPD stop-and-frisk campaign was overruled and subsequently reinstated by a three-judge panel of the U.S. Court of Appeals in 2013. It was ultimately scaled back under first-term New York City mayor Bill de Blasio, who had previously posed a grim forecast of where the country was heading with respect to singling out minorities for questionable searches and racial profiling. Obviously, there is reason to acknowledge that the change in NYPD policing strategy is helpful. However, black parents must stand their ground and continue talking to their children about how significant the differences are for a black child growing up in urban America. For them, there are few choices, and therefore it is a parental duty to have that frank discussion, and to routinely remind black and minority children to avoid situations that could, without warning, turn dangerous. Regrettably topping the list are encounters with police officers.

After the Zimmerman verdict, what became clear is that the parental conversation has to take into account that, because of the attitude of many in the general population, black children need to understand that when dealing with police officers, they must follow a prescribed attitude and behavior, and that straying from it could trigger a life-altering event. The brutal beating of Rodney King, the injustice related to the Central Park Five, the killing of Trayvon Martin, and countless other racially provoked and inexplicable incidents have morphed into a reality that black children are required to grasp. That reality clearly says that blacks, when approached not only by duly sworn law enforcement officers but also by white private citizens, must conform to what is deemed as a nonthreatening posture. Having to do so is, in my opinion, a contemporary variation reminiscent of the submission of blacks in a pre–civil rights South.

The fact that this has become a necessity for people of color makes clear that dealing with the fallout from racial profiling is crucial. However, in order to do so, the battle for equal treatment must be taken to the lawmakers who have time and again supported the unjust treatment of people based on the color of their skin. A major component of the stratagem to put an end to racial profiling has to start with reminding voters that it is their tax dollars that pay for the discriminatory treatment of minorities and the downtrodden.

It is difficult to accept that black children must be taught, from the time that they learn to speak, that their skin color is a liability that increases their exposure to perilous situations, and one that whites are not as likely to face. Many African American parents are horrified as they struggle to come to terms with the fact that their children must learn to protect themselves from bad guys who terrorize the communities where they live, and in addition, the insidious individuals that in uniform pose as good guys, yet are in actuality unfettered in their making of assumptions related to character and intent, based solely on the color of a person's skin.

According to an analysis conducted by the New York Civil Liberties Union (NYCLU) related to the NYPD's stop-and-frisk program, black parents and people of color have real reason for concern. For example, data from the NYCLU analysis confirmed that in 2012, police stopped New Yorkers 532,911 times. Of those stopped, 473,644, or 89 percent, were totally innocent; 284,229, or 55 percent of those detained, were black; 165,140, or 32 percent, were Latino; and 50,366, or 10 percent, were white.

The National Urban League, (NUL), the National Association for the Advancement of Colored People (NAACP), and the Nation of Islam are among the organizations that are qualified, by virtue of their history and reputation of service to urban communities, to assist in guiding minorities through what are perilous times, especially for black males. Now more than ever, the NUL, NAACP, and Nation of Islam are needed to contend with the polarizing effect that events like the Zimmerman acquittal are having throughout urban America. The services of these and other organizations, which have the expertise to demonstrate to people of color what they should do, and how to behave if stopped by police officers or confronted by individuals like Zimmerman that may harbor preconceived notions about them, unfairly based on the color of their skin, should be utilized.

While it is difficult to come to terms with, until progress is made in our courts to overturn unlawful practices like detaining, questioning, and searching innocent people because of their skin color, incidents like the one that cut short the life of a 17-year-old boy walking home from the store are bound to happen again.

If not for a change in leadership in New York City, the stop-and-frisk program would have likely continued and its use increased. Remember that in November 2013 came the shocking decision by a Second Circuit appellate court not only to grant a stay in Judge Shira A. Scheindlin's order to discontinue the controversial stop-and-frisk program, but to also remove her from the case. In reversing Scheindlin's decision, according to the Daily KOS, the appellate court also reprimanded Judge Scheindlin, saying that she "ran afoul" of the judiciary's code of conduct by compromising the "appearance of partiality."[21] This, according to Fox News, was due "in part because of a series of media interviews and public statements responding publicly to criticism of the court."[22] Following the reversal of Judge Scheindlin's order, then NYPD commissioner Raymond Kelly said, "This is indeed an important decision for all New Yorkers and for the men and women of the NYPD who work very hard day in and day out to keep this city safe ... I have always been, and I haven't been alone, concerned about the partiality of Judge [Shira] Scheindlin and we look forward to the examination of this case—a fair and impartial review of this case based on the merits."[23]

As it turns out, the 2013 New York City mayoral race became the determining factor related to stop-and-frisk. Democratic candidate Bill de Blasio campaigned in opposition of stop-and-frisk, while Republican hopeful Joe Lhota strongly supported the provocative program. After winning the election and becoming mayor, one of the first things that de Blasio did was to put the NYPD stop-and-frisk program on hold. In a statement countering the position of former New York mayor Michael Bloomberg, de Blasio, when referring to the controversial policing strategy in a Brooklyn news conference, said, "We believe these steps will make everyone safer," and "This will be one city where everyone rises together, where everyone's rights are protected."[24]

It is not only organizations, but also individuals that recognize the importance of boldly interceding to help protect black youngsters and to keep them safe in their own communities. Many are feverishly working to educate them and to teach coping skills that will aid in helping them through difficult situations. This is crucial, because finding ways to keep them off the street while instilling in them the realities related to how they are viewed by some segments of society, including members of the law enforcement community, is of the utmost importance. Organizations involved in this effort understand that getting across to young black people that, when confronted with a perilous situation such as being detained by police officers, the fundamentals and survival instinct are necessary. For example, a longtime friend, who is the father of a very bright and athletically gifted 19-year-old African American college student, shared with me that he has instructed his son, if at a social gathering, whether on campus or otherwise, to use his common sense and, for the sake of safety, always stay with a group of friends.

Salome Thomas-EL, author with Cecil Murphey of the best-selling book *I Choose to Stay* (with a foreword penned by Arnold Schwarzenegger), has been on the front lines doing things that offer children that live in urban America alternatives to the streets. Thomas-EL is a multiple award-winning educator, awardee of *Philadelphia Magazine*'s "Best Philadelphian," and a regular on the *Dr. Oz* show. The show's host, Dr. Mehmet Oz, said this about his friend and collaborator: "Principal EL is a superstar educator who is revolutionizing how we teach kids and is helping me motivate America to live right now."[25]

Principal EL, as he is affectionately known, refused to leave the inner city, and instead chose to stay and to interest the children of Philadelphia in the game of chess. Principal EL says, "Unfortunately, most of our nation's urban and rural students won't have the same opportunities as my chess players because, as a general rule, we don't teach our children to think critically or to think ahead. We don't teach them to use logic and reason or to consider rewards and consequences before they make decisions."[26] It's not necessary to read between the lines to understand what Principal EL is referring to, and that his reasoning is similar to the struggle and anxiety that minority parents are confronted with when raising children, especially young black men. It is not only something that I identify with as a parent, but I can recall my parents talking to me about it in my early teens. Likewise, when it was time to have the conversation with my sons, I was very candid and needed to be, because during their elementary school years, they attended private or predominantly white schools and were not as acquainted with the urban landscape. That said, they had been to an extent sheltered, and they had no idea of how their world would change as they matured and were perceived differently by society.

The abundance of cautions to minority children is troubling, and it strongly points toward the need for parents to instill in their children ways of staying safe, by being clear about boundaries and behavior. For instance, author and award-winning filmmaker Sarah Burns, in the amazing documentary *The Central Park Five*—which she made with her father, famed documentarian Ken Burns—examines the turbulent aftermath of what has come to be known as one of the most unjust and tarnishing examples of New York's criminal justice system. Beginning with details of the

horrendous April 20, 1989, rape and beating of a young white female jog-
ging in Central Park, brutalized within inches of her life, Burns goes on to
focus on the arrests of five teenagers of African American and Latino
descent who would later confess to the atrocious crime, yet almost immediately recant their confessions. That all-important confession ultimately led
to them being tried as adults and serving years in prison for a crime in
which there were no witnesses or DNA evidence. Burns's chilling film
brings back memories of the frenzied media blitz, public panic, and political overreach synonymous with this stunning and flagrant miscarriage of
justice. Moreover, Burns points up how the undeniable divide between
the races, the economically downtrodden, and the criminal justice system,
factored into the rush to judgment.

Further proof of where the deterioration and growing divide between
classes, ethnic groups, and law enforcement has brought us is discussed in
Michelle Alexander's controversial book, *The New Jim Crow: Mass
Incarceration in the Age of Colorblindness.* Alexander, an associate professor
of law at Stanford Law School, celebrated civil rights attorney, and legal
scholar, is the winner of the 2011 NAACP Image Award. In the straightforward exploration of the issue that is considered by some as a call to
action, Alexander reasons that:

> We have not eradicated the racial caste system in America; we have
> simply redesigned it. In today's "post-racial" society, nearly half of the
> nation's young black men are behind bars, on parole, or on proba-
> tion. And though, Jim Crow laws have been abolished, once a person
> is labeled a felon, old forms of prejudice-employment and housing
> discrimination, exclusion from jury service, and the denial of the
> right to vote, of educational opportunity, and of public benefits such
> as food stamps-become legal. As a criminal, you have scarcely more
> rights, and arguably less respect, than a black man living in
> Alabama at the height of Jim Crow.[27]

In his 2010 book, *The Condemnation of Blackness: Race, Crime, and the
Making of Modern Urban America,* author and director of the Schomberg
Center Khalil G. Muhammad, going back to the 1890s, discusses the
misnomer and invention of black criminality in America. Muhammad
skillfully gives an account of the how the erroneous notion of black criminality began with what is considered one of the most in-depth analyses of
the subject. Muhammad examines the notion of black criminality in urban
America, stating that, "The link between race and crime is as enduring
and influential in the twenty-first century as it has been in the past.

Violent crime rates in the nation's biggest cities are generally understood as a reflection of the presence and behavior of the black men, women, and children who live there. The U.S. prison population is larger than at any time in the history of the penitentiary anywhere in the world. Nearly half of the more than two million Americans behind bars are African Americans, and an unprecedented number of black men will likely go to prison during the course of their lives. These grim statistics are well known and frequently cited by white and black Americans; indeed for many they define black humanity."[28]

America's minorities and the underclass have always faced an uphill battle. However, given what has been proven time and again to be true in contemporary society, as it relates to the specific treatment of black males in America, the use of drastic measures must be thought out. However, considering that the origins of condemning black males, according to scholars like Burns, Muhammad, Thomas, Alexander, and others go back for more than a century, the precautions that are now integral to bringing up black children do not appear extreme.

NOTES

1. George Orwell, quoted in http://message.snopes.com/showthread.php?t=13173 (accessed October 30, 2014).

2. Noah Isackson, with additional research by Matt Schur, "Garry McCarthy under the Gun," *Chicago Magazine*, July 5, 2012, http://www.chicagomag.com/Chicago-Magazine/August-2012/Garry-McCarthy-Under-the-Gun/ (accessed October 24, 2014).

3. Monique Garcia, "House Sends Quinn Social Media Mob Action Bill," *Chicago Tribune*, May 10, 2013, http://www.chicagotribune.com/news/local/breaking/chi-house-sends-quinn-social-media-mob-action-bill-20130510,0,7680778.story (accessed October 3, 2013).

4. John Kass, "Kass: Police Patrolling Social Media to Curb Gang Violence," *Chicago Tribune*, April 7, 2014, http://articles.chicagotribune.com/2014-05-07/news/ct-social-media-kass-met-0507-20140507_1_social-media-gang-violence-new-unit (accessed May 15, 2014).

5. Angalia Bianca, CeaseFire Illinois supervisor, January 17, 2014.

6. Ibid.

7. Adam Hudson, "A Black Man Is Killed in the U.S. Every 28 Hours by Police," May 31, 2013, http://www.occupy.com/article/black-man-killed-us-every-28-hours-police (accessed October 20, 2013).

8. http://mxgm.org/operation-ghetto-storm-2012-annual-report-on-the-extrajudicial-killing-of-313-black-people/ (accessed October 30, 2014).

9. Hal Dardick and James Byrne, "Aldermen Call for Burge Reparations," *Chicago Tribune*, October 17, 2013, http://articles.chicago tribune.com/2013-10-17/news/ct-met-chicago-city-council-1017-20131017 _1_burge-victims-police-torture-torture-victims (accessed October 21, 2013).

10. Jeremy Gorner, *Chicago Tribune*, April 12, 2012.

11. Quoted in Julia Dahl, "Hot and Bothered: Experts Say Violent Crime Rises with the Heat," CBSNews.com, July 6, 2012, http://www .cbsnews.com/8301-504083_162-57467814-504083/hot-and-bothered -experts-say-violent-crime-rises-with-the-heat/ (accessed October 21, 2013).

12. Ibid.

13. Ibid.

14. Quoted in Jen Sabella, "Chicago Violence and Weather: The Connection between Warm Days and Murder in Chicago," *Huffington Post*, June 20, 2010, http://www.huffingtonpost.com/2010/04/20/chicago -violence-and-weat_n_544619.html (accessed October 23, 2013).

15. Ibid.

16. Jessica D'Onofrio and Paul Meincke, "City to Challenge Anthony Abbate Verdict as $850K Is Awarded in Bartender Beating Civil Trial," November 14, 2012, http://abclocal.go.com/wls/story?id=8884926 (accessed October 24, 2013).

17. Jordan Flaherty, "Chilling Accounts Revealed during Danziger Trial," *New Orleans Tribune*, http://www.tribunetalk.com/?p=901 (accessed October 27, 2013).

18. Ibid.

19. "Judge Cites DOJ Scandal to Void New Orleans Police Convictions for Katrina Deaths," http://beforeitsnews.com/politics/2013/09/judge-cites -doj-scandal-to-void-new-orleans-police-convictions-for-katrina-deaths -2551796.html (accessed October 27, 2013).

20. Anthony Stanford, "Zimmerman Trial All about Race," July 16, 2013, http://posttrib.chicagotribune.com/search/22134408-418/striking -the-balance-between-security-individual-rights.html#.VImlRKYqlMw (accessed October 27, 2013).

21. "Breaking: Second Circuit Reinstates Stop and Frisk, Reprimands and Removes Judge Scheindlin: Updates," Daily KOS, October 31, 2013, http://www.dailykos.com/story/2013/10/31/1252144/-BREAKING-2nd -Circuit-Reinstates-Stop-Frisk-Reprimands-and-Removes-Judge-Scheindlin# (accessed November 4, 2013).

22. "Federal Appeals Court Blocks Ruling on NYC Stop and Frisk Program," May 28, 2014, http://www.foxnews.com/us/2013/10/31/

federal-appeals-court-blocks-ruling-on-nyc-stop-and-frisk-program/ (accessed October 24, 2014).

23. Daniel Prendergast, Georgett Roberts, and Josh Saul, "NYPD Commissioner Ray Kelly Hails Stop-and-Frisk Decision," *New York Post*, October 31, 2013, http://nypost.com/2013/10/31/nypd-commissioner-ray -kelly-hails-stop-and-frisk-decision/ (accessed November 4, 2013).

24. Daniel Beekman, Annie Karni, and Ginger Adams Otis, "Mayor de Blasio Announces New York's Stop-and-Frisk Appeal Is on Hold," *New York Daily News*, January 30, 2014, http://www.nydailynews.com/new -york/new-york-stop-fighting-stop-and-frisk-article-1.1596610 (accessed June 24, 2014).

25. The Principal website, http://principalel.com/ (accessed June 24, 2014).

26. Salome Thomas-EL, "Chess: The Best Move for Students," *Education Week*, September 26, 2012, http://www.edweek.org/ew/articles/ 2012/09/26/05el.h32.html?qs=Salome+Thomas-El (accessed June 30, 2014).

27. Michelle Alexander, *The New Jim Crow: Mass Incarceration in the Age of Colorblindness*, New Press, 2012.

28. Khalil Gibran Muhammad, *The Condemnation of Blackness: Race, Crime, and the Making of Modern Urban America*, Harvard University Press, 2010.

6

❖

Department of Justice
Investigations

"No law is stronger than is the public sentiment where it is to be enforced."[1]

Some wonder if it was an act of sensationalism when Bobby Constantino intentionally got himself arrested. We may never know, but whatever it was it amounted to something more than the proverbial 15 minutes of fame. Constantino, a former Boston assistant district attorney who is white, says that he did it in order to test the fairness of our judicial system. According to Constantino, it is a system that he deeply believed to be predicated on a fundamental premise of providing equal protection to every American citizen. Instead, what Constantino found might come as a shocking revelation to some; yet to many others, it came as no surprise, because they had personally experienced the inequality of law enforcement and the glaring and inherent contradiction of the American system of justice.

Appearing in the December 2013 *Atlantic Monthly* and aptly titled, "I Got Myself Arrested So I Could Look Inside the Justice System," reveals the explicit difference in the way that blacks and whites are viewed and treated, and in Constantino's case, by members of the NYPD. I stand with those who believe Constantino had previous knowledge of the bias and genuinely felt a need to expose what he perceived as a flagrant pattern of inequity existing at the most basic level of the criminal justice system.

So, in the spring of 2012, Constantino began research to determine if the police treatment in a Brooklyn neighborhood called Brownsville was unbiased in accord with his belief that everyone is treated equally under the law. Constantino selected Brownsville, a community where police officers had detained 14,000 residents 52,000 times in a four-year period, in order to determine if law enforcement would respond to a white man dressed as a professional, in a suit and tie, as they had responded to thousands of others, who had been stopped and in some cases arrested for similar infractions of the law.

However, it turned out to be an arduous effort for Constantino to get himself arrested, even as he committed obvious criminal acts while NYPD officers looked on. Constantino said that in spite of the fact that he'd spent a number of years as a resident of neighborhoods similar to Brownsville, the police had never stopped him, and never seemed to view him with any hint of noticeable suspicion. Given his past personal experience with the NYPD, or lack thereof, Constantino concluded that he would have to come up with something exceptional to get the attention of the police, in order to experience the judicial system from the vantage point of the accused.

Constantino eventually managed to get himself arrested, and in the *Atlantic Monthly* piece, he tells exactly what it took to do so. Ironically, upon leaving the courthouse following his misdemeanor sentencing, Constantino reflected on it: "I noticed that there were some words carved into the façade of the building. It was a quote from Thomas Jefferson, describing one of the 'essential principles' of American democracy: 'Equal and exact justice to all men, of whatever state of persuasion.'"[2]

Many of those victimized as a result of inherent biases of the American criminal justice system are not surprised by Constantino's experience, and perceive, as I do, Thomas Jefferson's assertion as the utterance of a hypocritical slave owner and architect of a racially biased system of inequality. Having said that, if the readers were shocked by what Constantino found, then they have ignored what has been long alleged to exist within the American legal system by minorities, the economically disadvantaged, and the mentally ill. In fact, the ramping of investigations conducted by the Department of Justice (DOJ) under the Obama administration into claims of police misconduct, brutality or criminal behavior by police officers point to a pattern of systemic inequality, deficiencies, and a demonstrative failure of law enforcement agencies to adhere to their prescribed policies and training, especially as it related to the treatment of minorities.

DOJ's investigation into the New Orleans Police Department (NOPD) uncovered confusion, politics, and police spiraling out of control in response to the repercussion caused by Hurricane Katrina. The situation was exacerbated by a lack of police supervision that produced mayhem and a generally disastrous outcome. The common thread that runs through 5 of the 17 DOJ investigations examined center on nonadherence to established policing procedures. In its official report of the NOPD and other law enforcement agencies, the DOJ offered evidence that a biased, and in some cases sinister, culture has permeated law enforcement agencies throughout the country.

When the DOJ launches an investigation into a local law enforcement agency, the decision to do so and the subsequent action taken affect not only the organization under the DOJ's scrutiny, but also local politics. It can, of course, also create anxiety for the citizens who depend on their police department to protect them. Therefore, it is understandably difficult for one to fathom the possibility that the very people who are sworn to serve and protect have been accused, and in some instances proven guilty or complicit, in acts of police misconduct, brutality, and criminality.

The invasive nature of a DOJ investigation is one that tends to drag on, to create fear and anxiety, and, over time, to erode the morale of rank-and-file police departments. As it would in any facet of the criminal justice system, the mere specter of wrongdoing brings a sense of profound pressure that is difficult to deal with, and impossible to ignore. This is particularly true in situations where police officers are alleged to have violated the law and are placed on paid or unpaid leave pending the outcome of an internal investigation. If proven baseless, the issue can be stricken from the officer's record. However, if the charges alleged are proven true and the police officer is disciplined or fired, the circumstances can produce extraordinary difficulty, including a weakening of the underpinnings of the criminal justice system that trickles down to police commands that are left to deal with the aftermath and cleanup.

It is also often the case that elected officials are affected by DOJ's presence and are immediately concerned with how it will impact their constituencies and whether, at the end of the day, they will have to share responsibility for proven infractions related to police misconduct or biased treatment toward citizens. However, it is the day in, day out cloud of suspicion hanging over the heads of the police hierarchy that could, depending on the outcome of the DOJ investigations, determine if the officers have participated in acts of misconduct, nonadherence to the law and the oath that they are sworn to uphold, that produce enormous anxiety for all involved.

According to a PBS *Frontline* report in 2011, there were 17 active DOJ investigations of law enforcement agencies underway. In New Orleans, alleged unlawful activity by police officers in the wake of Katrina resulted in charges associated with the suspicious nature of police shootings by NOPD officers. Pro Publica reported that according to the DOJ, the NOPD had fostered an environment of "systematic violations of civil rights." In the 158-page report, the Justice Department's Civil Rights division said that the NOPD "has been largely indifferent to widespread violations of law and policy by its officers."[3]

The effect of the DOJ report was beyond stunning and potentially ruin-ous to the careers of the officers directly accused as well as those of some members of the NOPD pecking order. The NOPD, along with the 16 other law enforcement agencies being investigated by the DOJ for charges ranging from violations of civil rights to claims of police corruption, were commented on by Assistant Attorney General for Civil Rights Thomas Perez, who in a statement before the Senate Judiciary Committee when referring to the DOJ's investigation, said:

We prosecuted the most high profile incident of police misconduct since the Rodney King incident, securing the convictions of five New Orleans Police Department officers for their roles in a shooting on the Danziger Bridge in the wake of Hurricane Katrina that killed two civilians and wounded four. Five additional officers pled guilty to related charges.

The Division has 17 open pattern or practice investigations of law enforcement agencies, more than at any time in the Division's his-tory, including our extensive and comprehensive reviews of the New Orleans Police Department and the Puerto Rico Police Department.[4]

What follows are the synopses of several DOJ investigations into claims of police misconduct, wrongdoing, brutality, and civil rights violations. While they are troubling on a number of levels, a closer look at the DOJ's investigation of police departments and the culture that exist within some law enforcement organizations makes it difficult to argue against the existence of a troubled law enforcement culture.

The findings related to the DOJ investigations rank among the most egregious in recent memory. They illustrate why, in the eyes of the American public, confidence in our law enforcement agencies—and, in the minds of some, the entire criminal justice system—is in decline. This is not to suggest that the finding related to the police organizations under investigation is proof positive of a systemic failure of law enforcement in America. However, many are unwilling to trust police officers and a criminal justice system in which there is substantial evidence of misconduct, collusion, and outright criminality.

These and other allegations of police misconduct and various acts of wrongdoing forecast an escalation in the number of DOJ investigations of law enforcement agencies, as police departments come under fire brought about by the public's demand for answers and action. What appears to be undeniably true is that police shootings across the country, and nefarious activities investigated by the DOJ, reflect that problems are not necessarily systemic, but in some instances are acts perpetrated by rogue police officers. Nonetheless, given the public's anxiety along with the campaign waged against police in urban America, the conclusion is that there is indeed reason for concern and oversight.

NEW ORLEANS POLICE DEPARTMENT (NOPD)

The DOJ investigation into six incidents of questionable police shootings after Hurricane Katrina can be interpreted as a magnification of the divide and distrust that some have toward police officers and law enforcement organizations.

In what is fittingly referred to as the "chaotic aftermath" of Hurricane Katrina, four citizens were killed and four others wounded. Claims of civil rights violations were followed by charges of a concealment of evidence that pointed to the involvement of the NOPD command as it relates to the 2005 shootings of unarmed civilians. What resulted was believed to have been an overdue federal investigation into a long history of allegations by civilians and community leaders that a mob culture existed within the NOPD. The claims had been made consistently, and well before the NOPD had come to the attention of the nation as a result of the horrific news reports and images of Hurricane Katrina's devastation. However, the storm and escalating allegations connecting NOPD officers to the melee, and acts of criminality, could no longer be ignored. For instance, according to one official source, the New Orleans Tourism Marketing Corporation, pre–Hurricane Katrina claims of police brutality and misconduct by NOPD officers was nothing new. It reported that, "By the late 80s and early 90s, scandal started to hit the department and more than 60 officers were charged in a variety of crimes between 1992 and 1995."[5]

It began as sympathy for the masses of New Orleanians affected by the monstrous storm, but the tide soon turned. The ensuing calamity, rioting, stories of women and children being raped, and looting on a grand scale resulted in mobs of vigilantes roaming the streets of New Orleans, committing violent acts against unarmed citizens. Adding to that—and, some say, prompting the confusion and bedlam—were erroneous reports from government and law enforcement officials, including NOPD police superintendent Eddie Compass, who was among those named in a blame game that also included former New Orleans mayor Ray Nagin and Louisiana governor Kathleen Blanco. The trio was blamed for the disorganization and general unpreparedness of the city and state to respond to the catastrophic storm.

For their part, Blanco and Nagin were harshly criticized for their inaction in calling for a mass evacuation within 48 hours of the dire warnings issued by the National Hurricane Center (NOAA). Blanco in particular was deemed as being responsible for waiting too long to call for the deployment of 40,000 National Guard troops, something perceived by many as an action that would have helped to prevent the out-of-control situation that led to the death and suffering of innocent Crescent City residents.

Interviewed by NBC's Lisa Myers, the governor admitted that after assuring citizens and supporting agencies that things were under control, she should have made the call to evacuate earlier, when there was still time. What is clear is that efforts were being made to shift responsibility from one official to the next. Eventually, Federal Emergency Management Agency (FEMA) director Michael Brown would be saddled with failure in its responsibility and mission to, "support our citizens and first responders to ensure that as a nation we work together to build, sustain and improve our capability to prepare for, protect against, respond to, recover from and mitigate all hazards."[6]

In the end, the missteps by government officials may have contributed to the deteriorating conditions in the days before and after Hurricane Katrina. However, the five NOPD officers who entered guilty pleas associated with conspiracy would be hard pressed to connect governmental inaction to the accusations against them and the alleged NOPD attempt to cover up the travesty. Meanwhile, a half dozen other NOPD officers were indicted on charges related to the September 2, 2005, attempted murder of Donnell Herrington and the killing of Henry Glover. As lawlessness spread to the ranks of those sworn to serve and protect, the following day, Danny Brumfield was killed by a shotgun blast to the back. Subsequently, in what is infamously known as the Danziger Bridge shootings, on September 5, 2005, James Brissette and Ronald Madison were killed, and several others were wounded. Five of the officers accused of participating were convicted of felonious deeds and misconduct occurring in the aftermath of Hurricane Katrina.

Onlookers perceived what occurred in New Orleans in 2005 as a criminal enterprise, and pressed federal officials for a DOJ probe of the NOPD. With six other officers indicted on charges that included the murder of two unarmed civilians, and obstruction-of-justice indictments in connection with the Danziger Bridge incident, the DOJ eventually decided to conduct an investigation into the NOPD. The outcome, while astounding to some New Orleanians came as no surprise.

The DOJ investigation commenced nearly five years after Hurricane Katrina in May 2010 and lasted until March 2011. The findings of the investigation were detailed in a March 16, 2011, report presented by the U.S. Department of Justice, Civil Rights Division. The report revealed serious findings related to NOPD policing procedures. Among the most serious and unfavorable findings and practices were patterns of unconstitutional conduct, such as the prevalent nature of the NOPD's use of force deemed by the DOJ as "unreasonable force in violation of the Constitution and NOPD policy."

As it relates to discriminatory policies, the DOJ found reasonable cause to believe that the "NOPD engages in a pattern or practice of discriminatory policing in violation of constitutional and statutory law. Discriminatory policing occurs when police officers and departments unfairly enforce the law, or fail to enforce the law based on characteristics such as race, ethnicity, national origin, sex, religion, or LGBT status." In summarizing its assessment of the NOPD the DOJ found:

- Reasonable cause to believe that patterns and practices of unconstitutional conduct and/or violations of federal law occurred in several areas, including,
- Use of excessive force;
- Unconstitutional stops, searches and arrests;
- Biased policing, including:
- Racial and ethnic profiling and lesbian, gay, bi-sexual and transgender (LGBT) discrimination;
- A systemic failure to provide effective policing services to persons with limited English proficiency; and
- A systemic failure to investigate sexual assaults and domestic violence.
- The Justice Department also found a number of long-standing and entrenched practices within NOPD that caused or contributed to these patterns or practices of unconstitutional conduct, including:
- Failed systems for officer recruitment, promotion and evaluation;
- Inadequate training;

- Inadequate supervision;
- Ineffective systems of complaint intake, investigation and adjudication;
- A failed "Paid Detail" system;
- Failure to engage in community oriented policing;
- Inadequate officer assistance and support services; and
- Lack of sufficient community oversight.[7]

In spite of overwhelming evidence of civil rights violations within the NOPD in 2013, U.S. district judge Kurt Engelhardt, in a startling move, overturned the conviction of five of the former NOPD officers. In a scathing 129-page decision, Judge Engelhardt granted the officers' request for a new trial, saying that federal prosecutors had secretly used the Internet to post negative information about the officers, thereby depriving them of their right to a fair trial. In granting the officers' request, Engelhardt stated that, "Re-trying this case is a very small price to pay in order to protect the validity of the verdict in this case, the institutional integrity of the Court, and the criminal justice system as a whole."[8]

The ruling meant that the verdicts had been temporarily set aside, and that the four officers accused of firing at civilians on the Danziger Bridge, in the frenzied wake of Hurricane Katrina, and a fifth who had been charged with participating in covering up the crime, would be granted a new trial. Judge Engelhardt's ruling dealt a tremendous blow to the DOJ and was, at the very least considered a setback to the agency that had for a quarter century endeavored to expose misconduct within the NOPD. But it did not end there, because Engelhardt focused his ire on two federal prosecutors in particular who had allegedly played a role in the anonymous online besmirching of the accused officers on the *New Orleans Times-Picayune* website. In a very terse statement, Engelhardt said, "The government's actions, and initial lack of candor and credibility thereafter, is like scar tissue that will long evidence infidelity to the principles of ethics, professionalism, and basic fairness and common sense necessary to every criminal prosecution, wherever it should occur in this country."[9]

In response to Engelhardt's ruling, the DOJ released a statement: "We are reviewing the decision and considering our options."[10] However, the reality is that the extent to which the public's trust had been damaged, first by the egregious criminal charges against members of the NOPD and followed by the scandalizing overturning of their convictions, based on the alleged underhanded tactics of the highest law enforcement agency in the land, can only contribute to the public's distrust of the entire system.

PUERTO RICO POLICE DEPARTMENT (PRPD)

In its September 2011 report, the DOJ indicated that its investigation of the PRPD had revealed a pattern suggesting that PRPD officers had participated in repetitive practices that included excessive force in violation of the Fourth Amendment; unreasonable force and other misconduct designed to suppress the exercise of protected First Amendment rights; and unlawful searches and seizures in violation of the Fourth Amendment. The DOJ elaborated in its detailed and blistering evaluation identifying patterns of serious violations by the PRPD:

> In addition to these findings, our investigation uncovered other deficiencies of serious concern. In particular, there is troubling evidence that PRPD frequently fails to police sex crimes and incidents of domestic violence, and engages in discriminatory policing practices that target individuals of Dominican descent in violation of the Fourteenth Amendment, the Safe Streets Act, and Title VI. At this time, we do not make a formal finding of a pattern and practice violation in these areas, in part because PRPD does not adequately collect data to evaluate these issues. However, we are quite concerned that PRPD lacks basic systems of accountability to ensure that all individuals are treated equally by PRPD officers, regardless of race, ethnicity, national origin, or sex as required by federal law. Furthermore, our investigation raises serious concerns that PRPD policies and practices are woefully inadequate to prevent and address domestic violence committed by PRPD officers. We find that these deficiencies will lead to constitutional violations unless they are addressed. PRPD's continued failure to keep necessary data in light of our findings and despite knowledge of these indicators of a very serious problem, may constitute a pattern and practice that violates federal law.[11]

PORTLAND, OREGON, POLICE DEPARTMENT (POPD)

In announcing its intent to investigate the POPD, the DOJ indicated that a marked increase in police shootings was the reason for the investigation. The DOJ investigation of the POPD was focused on claims of excessive force against the city's mentally ill population. In its September 12, 2012, 42-page report addressed to Portland mayor Sam Adams, the DOJ enumerated the serious concerns and findings regarding the law enforcement agency's adverse actions. In the summation, the DOJ noted the gravity of its findings:

> The use of force is an essential part of law enforcement; however, it must be guided by policy and limited by the protections of the United States Constitution. While most force used by officers in Portland is appropriate, we find reasonable cause to believe that POPD is engaging in a pattern or practice of using excessive force in encounters involving people with actual or perceived mental illness. The pattern or practice is manifested in the following ways:
>
> 1) Encounters between PPB officers and persons with mental illness too frequently result in a use of force when force is unnecessary or in the use of a higher level of force than necessary or appropriate, up to and including deadly force. We found instances that support a pattern of dangerous uses of force against persons who posed little or no threat and who could not, as a result of their mental illness comply with officers' commands. We also found that PPB employs practices that escalate the use of force where there were clear earlier junctures when the force could have been avoided or minimized. As described in greater detail below, example of this use of excessive force include a December 2010 incident when multiple officers resorted to repeated closed-fist punches and repeated shocking of a subject who was to be placed on a mental health hold.
>
> 2) In particular, we found that PPB officers use electronic control weapons ("ECWs" commonly referred to as "Tasers") in circumstances when ECW use is not justified or use ECWs multiple times when only a single use is justified in encounters with people with actual or perceived mental illness. We found instances that support a pattern of officers using multiple cycles of shock without waiting between cycles to allow the suspect to comply, or officer failing to utilize control tactics during ECW cycles to properly affect handcuffing without having to resort to repeated ECW shocks. Examples detailed below include an August 10 incident when an officer repeatedly shocked an unarmed, naked subject who, as it turned out, was experiencing a diabetic emergency.
>
> 3) In effectuating an arrest, officers are permitted to use only the level of force reasonably necessary to accomplish a legitimate government objective; however we found that PPB officers use more force than necessary in effectuating arrests for low-level offenses involving people who are or appear to be in mental health crisis.[12]

NEWARK, NEW JERSEY, POLICE DEPARTMENT (NPD)

A request made by the American Civil Liberties Union (ACLU) to the DOJ initiated the investigation into the policies and procedures of the NPD. A petition in which complaints by Newark citizens were filed against the law enforcement agency had prompted the ACLU's action. Rogue NPD officers whose misconduct and alleged abuse had been permitted by the NPD's command was central to the citizen petition.

In its September 9, 2010, petition, the New Jersey ACLU, through an analysis and identification of 407 cases of police misconduct occurring over a period of 2.5 years, provided the DOJ with instances of "police shootings, sexual assault, beatings of prisoners, false arrests, reckless high-speed driving, and discrimination and retaliation against NPD's own officers by their superiors. It also details almost 40 lawsuits resolved at a taxpayer cost of at least $4.8 million during those same 2.5 years, and describes almost 40 other misconduct lawsuits that are still pending in federal or state court."[13]

The ACLU asked on behalf of petitioners that the DOJ investigate the allegations of abuse and require that the NPD enforce the implementation of meaningful solutions. Atop the ACLU's request list were reforms of the NPD having to do with improvements within internal affairs, police disciplinary action, and independent monitoring of police. The petition also asked that the DOJ require that policies known to have worked in law enforcement agencies throughout the country be instituted by the NPD.

On May 9, 2011, the DOJ began its investigation of the NPD, covering alleged incidents and settlements occurring from January 1, 2008, until July 1, 2010. The DOJ's investigation was based on the ACLU's amended petition that claimed the following incidents had occurred:

- *1*: The number of serious Internal Affairs complaints upheld by Newark out of 261 filed in calendar years 2008 and 2009. The one sustained complaint alleged an improper search.
- *2.5*: The number of years covered by the ACLU-NJ's petition.
- *7.7*: The factor by which Newark's 2009 murder rate is higher than New Jersey's rate.
- *26*: The number of police departments the DOJ has formally investigated, entered into settlement agreements, or filed lawsuits since it was granted power to do so in 1994.
- *42*: The number of settled lawsuits against the NPD documented in the ACLU-NJ's petition.

- *43*: The number of years that spanned between the ACLU-NJ's first appeal for federal intervention of the troubled NPD in 1967 and its current appeal.
- *44*: The number of lawsuits in the ACLU-NJ's petition that were filed by citizens against the NPD alleging beatings, false arrests, death, theft, retaliation and other forms of intentional misconduct or negligence by police.
- *64*: The total number of lawsuits filed against the NPD documented in the ACLU-NJ's petition.
- *186*: The number of Internal Affairs cases that the NPD dropped from its Internal Affairs statistics between 2008 and 2009, providing the public with no information about the complaint outcomes, if any.
- *418*: The number of serious police abuse complaints documented in the ACLU-NJ's petition.
- *$4,800,000*: The minimum amount of dollars Newark paid out to settle lawsuits, including 13 claims of false arrests, 11 excessive force complaints, and seven internal affairs improprieties.
- *Priceless*: There is no way to quantify the price we all pay when the bond of trust unravels between a police department and the community it has sworn to protect and serve.[14]

SEATTLE POLICE DEPARTMENT (SPD)

At the conclusion of the DOJ investigation into a pattern of civil rights practices by the SPD, Seattle mayor Michael McGinn received the findings and recommendations in a letter. For the mayor of any municipality, such a letter can be, depending on the seriousness of the findings, career altering.

The joint DOJ investigation that included the U.S. Department of Justice, Civil Rights Division, and the U.S. Attorney's Office for the Western District of Washington was authorized by federal laws such as the Violent Crime Control and Law Enforcement Act of 1994, the Omnibus Crime Control and Safe Streets Act of 1968, and Title VI of the Civil Rights Act of 1964. As in the other investigations launched by the DOJ, federal laws allow for the filing of lawsuits to remedy patterns or practices carried out by law enforcement agencies that cause the intentional or nonintentional denial of an individual's rights, privileges, or immunities secured by the Constitution or laws of the United States.

In the case of the SPD, the DOJ investigation focused on allegations related to unlawful methods of policing that included excessive force and discriminatory policing procedures. The parameters of the DOJ investigation were discussed prior to issuance of the official report, wherein structural deficiencies were cited that worsened the activities of some SPD officers who were less experienced. In addition, a deficit in leadership, training, mentoring, and requisite oversight were believed to be contributing factors, and included in the DOJ's report.

The investigation of the SPD began in March 2011, when several highly publicized incidents involving SPD officers were caught on video. Among the occurrences captured was a fatal and seemingly unprovoked police shooting, a member of the SPD gang enforcement team threatening physical harm to a Latino man, and the brutal physical treatment of an African American man attempting to comply with an SPD officer's order to surrender. These incidents were believed to be proof positive of the existence of problems within the SPD. They along with public outcry were the cause for DOJ's decision to launch an investigation, and SPD's command did not escape unscathed. In fact, the DOJ's severely critical report concluded that the engagement of the department's chain of command at every level was the only way to remedy the problems identified in the DOJ report.

DOJ's investigation of the SPD concluded the existence of constitutional violations that suggested a pattern or practice of such incidents that were consistent enough to warrant a court-enforceable, written resolution accompanied by a timetable for completion by the SPD. The DOJ report continued, stating that compliance with its method for resolving the outstanding findings would "[i]mprove public confidence in the Department and enhance its ability to provide safety of all Seattle residents."[15]

While noting optimism and confidence in the SPD's commitment to resolve the issues, the DOJ's emphasis on the numerous systemic deficiencies that continued to exist despite reform efforts, placed considerable pressure on SPD's high command. For instance, one of the DOJ's findings cited the repeated violation of the Fourth Amendment of the U.S. Constitution, resulting from a pattern or practice of SPD officers using unnecessary or excessive force. The DOJ also pointed out that officers in some cases did not have adequate training as it relates to the appropriate use of deadly weaponry.

The findings and recommendations of the DOJ are nothing new, yet they serve to illustrate why there has been an erosion of public confidence in law enforcement at every level. Some law enforcement professionals perceive the DOJ's use of its investigative power as an overreach and an uncalled-for intrusion into SPD's effort to maintain law and order. However, an increasing number of Americans demand that their government do more to protect rights guaranteed by the Constitution.

NOTES

1. Abraham Lincoln, quoted in http://izquotes.com/quote/330557 (accessed November 11, 2013).

2. Bobby Constantino, "I Got Myself Arrested So I Could Look inside the Justice System," *Atlantic*, December 17, 2013, http://www.theatlantic .com/national/archive/2013/12/i-got-myself-arrested-so-i-could-look-inside -the-justice-system/282360/ (accessed January 1, 2014).

3. U.S. Department of Justice, *Investigation of the New Orleans Police Department*, March 16, 2011, http://www.justice.gov/crt/about/spl/nopd _report.pdf (accessed January 1, 2014).

4. Sarah Moughty, "17 Justice Dept. Investigations into Police Departments Nationwide," *Frontline*, September 20, 2011, http://www .pbs.org/wgbh/pages/frontline/criminal-justice/law-disorder/17-justice -dept-investigations-into-police-departments-nationwide/ (accessed November 11, 2013).

5. "History of the New Orleans Police Department," http://www .neworleansonline.com/pr/releases/releases/History%20of%20New%20 Orleans%20Police%20Department.pdf (accessed December 28, 2013).

6. "About the Agency," http://www.fema.gov/about-agency (accessed December 29, 2013).

7. U.S. Department of Justice, "Department of Justice Releases Investigative Findings Involving the New Orleans Police Department," March 17, 2011, http://www.justice.gov/opa/pr/2011/March/11-crt-342 .html (accessed December 29, 2013).

8. A. C. Thompson, "Danziger Bridge Convictions Overturned," ProPublica, September 17, 2013, http://www.propublica.org/nola/story/ danziger-bridge-convictions-overturned/ (accessed December 29, 2013).

9. Quoted in Juliet Linderman, "Judge Grants New Trial for Ex–New Orleans Police Officers Convicted in Notorious Danziger Bridge Slayings after Hurricane Katrina," NOLA.com/*The Times-Picayune* (New Orleans), September 17, 2013, http://www.nola.com/crime/index.ssf/ 2013/09/judge_grants_new_trial_for_ex-.html (accessed July 8, 2014).

10. Quoted in Allen Johnson Jr. and Margaret Cronin Fisk, "New Orleans Police Win New Trial in Danziger Bridge Case," Bloomberg, September 17, 2013, http://www.bloomberg.com/news/2013-09-17/new -orleans-police-win-new-tmrial-in-danziger-bridge-case.html (accessed July 8, 2014).

11. U.S. Department of Justice, *Investigation of the Puerto Rico Police Department*, September 5, 2011, http://www.justice.gov/crt/about/spl/ documents/prpd_exec_summ.pdf (accessed July 8, 2014).

12. http://www.justice.gov/crt/about/spl/documents/ppb_findings_9-12 -12.pdf (accessed July 8, 2014).

13. "Petition to Investigate the Newark Police Department," http:// www.aclu-nj.org/legaldocket/petitiontoinvestigatethene/ (accessed December 31, 2013).

14. "A Petition for Justice in the Newark Police," https://www .aclu-nj.org/theissues/policepractices/apetitionforjusticeinthene/ (accessed July 8, 2014).

15. U.S. Department of Justice, *Investigation of the New Orleans Police Department.*

7

A Saga of Police Corruption

"Corruption is nature's way of restoring our faith in democracy."[1]

A couple of years ago, I was honored when invited to the swearing-in ceremony of three police officers in my hometown, Aurora, Illinois. It was especially significant because one of the young men taking the oath that day grew up doors from me. Because of this, the ceremony was all the more moving. I had been invited by the Jones family, my neighbors of more than two decades and whose son Aaron, was among those being sworn in by Aurora Police Department (APD) chief Greg Thomas. It was an especially inspiring experience to watch this young man, whom I've known since he was about five years old, before he learned to ride a bicycle, taking the solemn oath to serve and protect. It occurred to me that from this day forward, Aaron would be on the front line, protecting and serving the citizens of the second-largest city in Illinois. As I watched the ceremony, my thoughts turned to how these three, filled with limitless promise, would on a routine basis confront danger, hostility, hopelessness, suspicion, and yet rarely a display of appreciation.

I was ecstatic when Chief Thomas cleared my interview of Aurora police rookie officer Jones. I was eager to talk with him about the decision to become a police officer and to ask what he thought the role of a police officer in contemporary society should be. Officer Jones responded with the same straightforwardness that has defined him since boyhood—poised, reflective, and sincere. Here is what Officer Jones had to say about what being a police officer means to him:

> I think that every young boy dreams of being an action movie star, and television shows such as *Cops* definitely help to fuel that dream. So growing up, I was somewhat torn between a law enforcement and military career. I knew that both would be fast paced, and would always keep me on my toes. After the tragedy of 9/11 I knew that I wanted to protect my loved ones more than ever before. One of the deciding factors came when watching [a] news broadcast as 2001 came to an end, at which point America was at war. I remember hearing the News Anchor announce the name of each solider that had lost their life during the war. Each name took only seconds to read, however the entire list lasted for close to an hour. It was at this point that I knew I wanted to return home at the end of each day to my loved ones. I was raised in the city that I now patrol, and have seen the city go through difficult points in which innocent citizens were gunned down in their own neighborhood because they were wearing the wrong color combination. I decided that I wanted to help change that. I told myself that when I have children of my own, I'd like for them to know that their father is working to make things safer for them.
>
> I am incredibly satisfied with my decision to become a police officer, and I gain a great sense of value in the work that I do. Most people do not understand the amount of judgment placed on police officers. From the instant that I put on my uniform, or even step into my squad car, I am instantly hated by a portion of society, despite the fact that they know nothing about me. Some people have the preconception that I gain pleasure in ruining someone's day, however this is not the case. My purpose, more than anything else, is to help the citizens of my city. When someone has an issue they cannot resolve, they contact 9-1-1, and reach a group of specialists trained to assist in the particular scenario. The nature of my job exposes me to the graphic horrors, and to my fellow citizens, in their darkest moments. My job is to remain level headed in order to best assist, and to serve my community.
>
> Then there is the important interaction within the community and the people that live in the neighborhoods. Many urban police departments are implementing or strengthening their presence with a variety of policing strategies. For example, community policing allows an officer the opportunity [to] become acclimated with the

people in the communities that they patrol. The officer is then able to build a rapport within the community, one that increases the efficiency of communication, and improves the response capability of law enforcement.

As far as the rapid advances in technology go they are crucial, and necessary to the function of law enforcement agencies. Technology is essential to the safety of law enforcement efforts worldwide. For example, when I encounter a subject, and gather pertinent information such as name, and date of birth, I relay this information to a dispatcher. The dispatcher can then conduct a search of the subject's criminal record, to discover any vital information that the officer may need to know. Such information includes whether the subject possesses a valid license, a warrant, whether the subject is considered missing, or whether the subject has a prior history of gang activity, being armed and dangerous, and countless other possibilities. Remarkable advances in technology make it possible for an officer to gather this information within a matter of seconds and can often mean the difference between life and death.[2]

Chances are that Officer Jones would have been considered a standout recruit by any police department. In the eyes of the law enforcement hierarchy, he possesses the sought-after qualities so vital to law enforcement agencies. In fact, Jones' idealism embodies the elements of what an overwhelming majority of newly recruited police officers possess. In spite of the fact that veteran police officers might consider the fresh perspective and enthusiasm of a rookie officer as naïveté, they would likely concede that it is the "right stuff" and embodies the aspirations that they once had, yet over the years has been transformed by reality.

Insiders will not be surprised, but others were shocked in 2012 when serious allegations were leveled against 12 highly esteemed U.S. Secret Service agents assigned to President Obama's security detail. The agents were accused of frolicking with prostitutes while on a presidential detail in Bolivia. Though denied by the administration, it is believed that their behavior may have potentially endangered the leader of the free world and put American security at risk. Deemed outrageous, elected officials condemned the dicey behavior, and the charges against the agents resulted in their dismissal.

The agents' behavior is thought to be nothing new and believed to be part of the U.S. Secret Service culture. A shocked American public struggled with the allegation that the Secret Service agents had participated in nefarious activities that could have jeopardized the homeland.

However, this pales in comparison to what nearly occurred during the second George W. Bush presidential administration. In fact, to contrast the buffoonery of a dozen Secret Service agents to the nomination of former New York City police commissioner Bernard Kerik to head the Department of Homeland Security (DHS) would be incredibly out of proportion. This is because Kerik's nomination represents one of the most chilling examples of criminal factions, penetrating the highest level of government and posing a direct threat to the American people.

In what onlookers perceived as a modern-day Horatio Alger story, Kerik worked his way up the incredibly politicized career ladder of New York City's take-no-prisoner politics. He began by working on the security detail of former New York mayor Rudolph Giuliani, and over time, Kerik was selected to head the New York Department of Corrections and was eventually credited with restoring order to the formerly infamous Riker's Island. It is believed that the widely viewed success in reestablishing stability at Riker's Island was the catalyst for Kerik being named NYPD commissioner. Kerik held this post until his nomination by President Bush to succeed Thomas J. Ridge as DHS secretary.

In spite of his impressive resume, the nomination of the former NYPD commissioner almost immediately received mixed political reviews. For instance, media reports of Kerik reaping stock-option windfalls, fraudulent apartment renovations, and a sexual affair with the publisher of his memoir, *Lost Son: A Life in Pursuit of Justice*, while married to his third wife, began to surface, and political resistance to Kerik's nomination as DHS secretary amplified. As pressure mounted, many speculated that in order to spare his mentor Giuliani not only tremendous political embarrassment, but also besmirching of Giuliani's image as "America's Mayor," Kerik withdrew his nomination for the cabinet-level post. The alarming news and facts that were later disclosed caused reverberations inside the Beltway. Instead of Kerik becoming a trusted member of President Bush's cabinet, the outcome was an indictment charging Kerik with tax evasion and lying to federal authorities. The former NYPD commissioner was subsequently sentenced to four years in a federal minimum-security prison.

Aside from the shocking blow to those who supported his nomination as DHS secretary, Kerik's fall from grace was extremely disheartening for the Republican Party. However, if not for the revved opposition to his nomination and intense scrutiny of the national media, the damage could have been far worse. Imagine if Kerik's nomination had not been derailed and that he had become DHS secretary. For starters, it could have created a potential risk to American security; and moreover, it could have affected the agency's ability to successfully perform its mission to prevent terrorism, secure our borders, and safeguard cyberspace. It is conceivable that individuals having knowledge of his involvement in criminal acts could have used the information against Kerik. The potential for blackmailing Kerik would have put at risk the DHS mission, U.S. security, and American lives.

The nomination and near appointment of Kerik was spun as an embarrassment, downplaying the potential and near-catastrophic exposure to the safety of the American public. Kerik as DHS secretary would have immediately become one of the most relied-upon members of the president's cabinet, bringing with him the potential for a number of troubling scenarios. As Kerik participated in criminal wrongdoing, exactly how the prospect of his appointment would have endangered the security of the homeland is difficult to gauge. However, in known and unknown ways, Kerik could have become a target of anti-American forces. Moreover, let's remember that had Kerik been sworn in before the revelations of his criminality came to light, the ramifications would have presented complexities across the board. What is clear is that the action taken to derail the nomination, and Kerik's decision to withdraw his name from consideration as DHS secretary, was once again used to convince the American people that things are under control; and that the highest levels of our government, because of its system of checks and balances, had avoided the taint by identifying and weeding out the criminal element. Moreover, the importance of getting this message out was one of political expediency. Still, others used the incident to prove that political influence, ambition, and, in this instance, the push to install Kerik had trumped what is by most accounts a normally rigorous vetting process designed to protect the American public.

So much about the realities of the criminal justice system is not known to the general public, and many put their trust and confidence in what they believe is the very capable hands of law enforcement professionals. However, due to the acceptance of a skillfully crafted criminal justice system façade, the warped underbelly of politics and its effect on the criminal justice system is rarely exposed. That said, widespread knowledge of the seamy side of the criminal justice system would do little to quell the public's anxiety or to appease astute politicians that appreciate the importance of the appearance of law and order. They know that their staying power is complexly linked to the peace of mind of Americans.

As do others, I believe that during the mid-1990s in Chicago and in other major urban centers, the crime-fighting blitz to combat gangs, drugs, and violence undertaken by law enforcement's upper echelon was primarily politically driven. This is not to say that the good of the people was not an intended by-product; but arguably, politics was the motivation. For instance, an extraordinary marshaling of an array of crime-fighting professionals, including the prosecutorial forces of the federal government combined with the might of local law enforcement agencies, said to unite in an effort to reduce crime and make inner-city neighborhoods safer, was more likely initiated to boost partisan political ambitions by using the war against crime as a key platform plank. As in the past and continuing today, politicians can either benefit from or suffer the consequences of efforts focused on eradicating crime.

While it is certainly true that the law-abiding residents of urban America long to see exacting measures being taken to rid their neighborhoods of the lawlessness perpetrated by violent drug-dealing gangbangers, increasingly people are arriving at the realization that the ulterior motive of a gargantuan collaborative law enforcement effort is multidimensional. For instance, there was certainly enough crime to substantiate CPD's 1992 crackdown on crime, when 934 homicides were committed in Chicago, just 36 shy of the record 970 slain in 1974. According to the *Chicago Tribune*, "Because 400,000 more people lived in the city in 1974, the murder rate was 30.6 per 100,000 residents. In 1992, the murder rate hit a record high of 33.7."[3] Most were said to have been black males who were victims of the mayhem and gang violence, generally linked to illicit drug sales and disputes over gang turf. Viewing it as anarchy, it was enough to move citizens to demand that something be done to decrease the violence and to hold accountable not only police officers, but also elected officials for failing to rid the city of the epidemic of drugs and violence.

Law enforcement–initiated tactics launched during the 1990s to combat rampant crime in urban communities were also necessary to give the appearance of the effectiveness of the law-and-order effort. Past initiatives, and those undertaken since, are intended to quell the angst of the public that they are not being safeguarded; however, people realize that this is not the case. Moreover, they also recognize that an alarming number of police officers have already violated, or will violate, their sworn oath to serve and protect. For a number of reasons, somewhere along the way, things fall apart, and unfortunately, the optimism present at the start of one's career is diminished by harsh reality and a combination of other factors. Indeed, many police officers, in spite of ever-present temptation, manage to adhere to their oath to the public, and they do so with professionalism and integrity. However, the simple truth is that others do not, and unfortunately, many become entangled in serious acts of brutality and corruption that violate the sacred pledge to protect the citizenry. Consequently, it not only ruins their careers and adversely impacts their families, but their action also adversely impacts entire communities and sullies the reputation of police departments.

In the mid-1990s, amid one of the most ambitious law-and-order campaigns in the history of the city of Chicago, perhaps the entire country, a former CPD Gang Crimes Unit officer, Sonia Irwin, found herself engulfed in—and, some believe, a victim—of the law enforcement crusade against gangs and violence. In what began as a chance encounter with an individual who had grown up in her community, Irwin made a series of adverse, career-ending, and life-altering decisions that are difficult to imagine.

In the interest of full disclosure, Irwin and I have been friends since childhood, growing up in the Chicago South Side working-class neighborhood known as Avalon Park. There was a time when we could not have imagined that drugs, gangs, and violence would infiltrate the peaceful place where we came of age. Yet, by the time we were teenagers, we began to witness the neighborhood's transformation and the introduction of gangs and violence. Similar to others who grew up in like circumstances, an awareness of the changing environment and the instinct necessary to survive was essential. This meant honing the skills necessary to hang on to one's fundamental principles and sense of value in the midst of a community undergoing rapid change. I can clearly remember an incident that proved our time of innocence had passed and our sense of security shaken. It occurred on May 17, 1969, when a street gang known as the Black P Stone Nation killed Michael Causher, a young man from our neighborhood. Causher was rumored to have been a member of a rival Chicago street gang known as the Disciples. Although he was not well known to us, the fact that Causher was killed just several miles away from our neighborhood was shocking. Word of Causher's demise spread quickly, and our safe, secure world suddenly changed.

The significance of Causher's murder for me was that it revealed to me the importance of surviving the blight of gangs and other sinister forces. Not long after Causher's death, I was walking home from school with several of my friends. Though we were not affiliated with a street gang, from a car window, a young man aimed a shotgun at us. Now fully aware of the danger that had invaded our community, we scattered, at breakneck speed in every direction, to escape what had been Causher's fate. I will never forget how we ran across a gravel lot, the dust rising from beneath our feet, as we scrambled to the safety of a comrade's home.

The significance of the survival instinct was not relegated to black males; it was also essential for females growing up in urban America. Some mastered a combination of charm, intellect, and femininity that would on many occasions insulate black males from physical harm. Irwin, who was smart, attractive, and determined, was incredibly adept at navigating both worlds, often looking out for friends who were not as proficient, when it came to dealing with the realities of our changing community and adapting to the radical societal transformation.

This eventually earned Irwin the respect of many and some say, most importantly, gang members who respected her savvy and fearlessness in the face of danger. Undoubtedly, it was Irwin's knack for piloting between worlds that made her an excellent CPD recruit and, down the road, gang crimes police officer. Ironically, in the end, it became a double-edged sword. While her ability to effectively interact with gang members was a tremendously important skillset as an officer on the tough streets of Chicago, circumnavigating the two may have been the very thing that led to a series of unwise choices that, during the law-and-order crackdown of the 1990s, were used to exemplify a crossing of the line and a violation of the sacred oath to serve and protect.

However, it was likely the complex dichotomy and very nature of career choice, aspiration, and survival instinct that in the end were key in lapses of judgment that caused Irwin to be named in a federal indictment. At arraignment, the federal prosecutor charged the former CPD gang crime police officer with aiding and abetting a multimillion-dollar gang drug operation. In what was, and is still, considered by some as an incredible overreach and a miscarriage of justice, the real aims, at least in part, were to quell fear in black communities and to boost the careers of politicians and criminal justice officials with what were sensational charges. It is hard to imagine that there was a better way to convince the public that Chicago's law enforcement apparatus was waging war on gangs and violence and, in doing so, was willing to take down one of its own. Irwin was found guilty and sentenced to federal prison, but the saga compels one to ask whether justice was served, or if an individual's life, environment, and experience were being judged and unfairly condemned.

Irwin's trouble became known when a *Chicago Tribune* article revealed that a 50-count federal indictment had been handed down accusing Larry Hoover, the leader of the notorious Chicago street gang the Gangster Disciples, who had already been convicted and imprisoned for ordering the murder of a drug dealer, and of engineering a drug operation from a prison telephone. According to the *Tribune* story, the indictment sought the forfeiture of $10 million in profits and, in addition to known members of the Gangster Disciples, delivered the shocking news that CPD officer Sonia Irwin was a coconspirator. When the article was published, Irwin had been recently reassigned from her duties as a gang crimes officer to a mass transit beat. The piece implied that

Irwin's role in the criminal enterprise, if any, was unclear. However, then Chicago Police superintendent Matt Rodriquez, referring to Irwin said, "Her involvement was known to us for a long time"; the statement strongly hinted that the CPD had been monitoring Irwin's activity for some time.

During the federal government's prosecution of Irwin, whose conviction came prior to 18 Gangster Disciple leaders that were on trial for the narcotics conspiracy and other drug-related offenses, it was revealed that the former police officer had been involved with gang leader Gregory "Shorty" Shell. He had been identified by law enforcement as the number-two person in command of the Gangster Disciples. However, what the public was not privy to was that Irwin had known Shell since the age of eight. Of course, the fact that Irwin had known Shell for many years does not excuse her severe lapse in judgment, or the fact that having any type of relationship with Shell had not only been an incredibly bad choice, but also invited speculation that she might have been involved with the criminal element. However, at the time of the trial, Irwin countered by saying because Shell was someone that she had known since childhood, the nature of the relationship was to guide Shell in a positive direction.

However, prior to encountering Shell, there is no doubt that Irwin had begun her career as a law enforcement officer with the same enthusiasm and idealism as young Officer Jones, and for that matter, any individual embarking on a new career related to their chosen profession. Unfortunately, in the end, the federal charges of aiding and abetting a criminal enterprise would bring to an end, for Irwin, what had been a very promising law enforcement career.

Two decades since the prosecution of Irwin, and following her release from federal prison in 2008, her staunch supporters, including me, continue to believe that her prosecution was a politically motivated, overly severe product of ambitious politicians, federal prosecutors, and a police force under enormous pressure to produce results. Moreover, the irony is that it occurred while the egregious misconduct and brutality ordered by the CPD's high command was in full swing. However, hell-bent on improving its image Cook County law-enforcement, CPD and federal prosecutors found Irwin a suitable sacrifice.

It's not that Chicago politicians and federal prosecutors were exaggerating the growth of gangs and drugs, because according to reports at the time, the Gangster Disciples, already comprised of 30,000 members, were rapidly growing and had expanded their nefarious operations to 28 states. According to the *Los Angeles Times*, the annual earnings derived from the gang's illicit activities was said to have been more than $100 million.[4] Not only that, but the gang was broadening its reach by infiltrating politics. As reported in a September 1, 1995, *Los Angeles Times* article, the Gangster Disciples were using proceeds from its highly sophisticated drug operation to finance a political action committee known as 21st Century V.O.T.E. (Voices of Total Empowerment). At the time, it was alleged that the Gangster Disciples were providing financial support for two members of the gang that, with gang proceeds, were able to force runoff elections for two Chicago city council aldermanic seats.

What is also true is that mayoral candidate Richard M. Daley had no choice but to run on his record of law and order that was based on an almost decade-long run as Cook County state's attorney. Yet, when it came to Burge and the alleged torture of criminal suspects, Daley dodged questions about what he knew and when he knew it. Still, in his first mayoral campaign in the late 1980s and reelection bid, Daley used his criminal justice credentials to take a stance against gangs and drugs. The strategy was found to be extremely effective, and exactly what residents of neighborhoods plagued by gang violence and open-air drug dealing wanted to hear from their elected officials. Meanwhile, theories like the one espoused by political scientist John Diulio in the 1990s, that "superpredators" were roaming the urban landscape committing unspeakable crimes, made the case brought by federal prosecutors against Irwin and the Gangster Disciples all the more salacious. Years later, Diulio's theory would prove to be incorrect, and he would distance himself from the hypothesis; but at the time, it was used to garner bipartisan support for a crackdown on crime across urban America. Given the overall effect of Diulio's concept, and its impact on the criminal justice system, it more than likely played a role in pragmatic politics that were advantageous to politicians and federal prosecutors connected to the sensationalized prosecution. There is also little doubt that the clampdown on gangs, drugs, and crime in general gave the appearance that the city's law enforcement community was proactively engaged in protecting citizens from the scourge of gangs and illicit drug sales. Still, there is a strong suspicion that Irwin's prosecution was needed to promote the notion of purging the CPD of wayward officers and that it was willing to go in whatever direction the evidence pointed, even if it meant bringing down one of its own to prove it. However, to Irwin's defense team and some onlookers, it appeared that Irwin's prosecution was not only excessive, but also politically motivated—as subterfuge for the sinister activities of a CPD high command that had lost control. What better way to convince citizens that things were under control than to indict known gangbangers and to make an example of a former gang crimes CPD officer? Therefore, alleging, indicting, and ultimately securing Irwin's conviction was indeed the perfect camouflage.

Though unsuccessful, the facts as presented by Irwin's defense team as well as those argued in a subsequent appeal are, to say the least, compelling. Undoubtedly Irwin's life experience navigating two worlds and a colossal lapse in judgment were significant factors in her conviction. The former officer and convicted felon knows that by blurring the line of law enforcement ethics, particularly consorting with any faction of the criminal element, was irresponsible and tempted the hands of fate. Furthermore, in spite of the fact that she was not engaged in the gang's nefarious acts and had nothing whatsoever to do with drug dealing, the fraternization with Shell discredited the trust conferred to her by the people of Chicago. Having said that, many believe that Irwin, aside from being a product of a complex environment and upbringing, was made the scapegoat. It is to my way of thinking circumstances that, if not for political ambition, a demanding public, and an individual who had walked among both worlds for her entire life, would not have occurred. The irony is that in a number of ways, Irwin became a victim of the criminal justice system, a system that must, from time to time, sacrifice one of its own in order to prove that the system is working and that all is well. What better way to accomplish this than to single out and to exploit the reckless decision of a police officer that has by his or her own admission crossed the proverbial line.

In his closing argument, attorney Rick Halpern, summarizing the case against his client, a defendant ensnarled in the Gangster Disciple trial spoke to the issue of the effect of one's environment saying, "We're not here to judge lifestyles," and "That's the way it was on the streets."[5]

In 1998, on appeal, Irwin's defense team in an attempt to overturn the conviction, sought relief from the U.S. 7th Circuit Court of Appeals in *USA v. Sonia Irwin*. The former gang crimes officer's legal counsel argued before circuit court judges Ripple, Manion, and Evans to have her conviction of aiding and abetting a drug conspiracy in violation of 21 U.S.C. section 846 overturned on two points, saying that, "[a]s a matter of law one cannot aid and abet a conspiracy by assisting the conspirators after they have made their unlawful agreement, at which point the crime of conspiracy is complete. Second, Irwin argues that the government's evidence was insufficient to support her conviction."[6]

Laying out the facts of the case, the defense first stated that the relationship between Irwin and Shell was not only unlikely, but that their lives intersecting was, on its face, implausible. Though childhood friends, Irwin had taken a path to a career in law enforcement, while

Shell had gone in an extreme and opposite direction, becoming the second-in-command of the Gangster Disciples, which dominated Chicago's street-level drug trade. Unthinkably, as adults, they began a relationship.

To understand the extent of the case against Irwin, and to determine if it had merit or was motivated by political and prosecutorial ambition, it is necessary to go back to the 1960s. Over four decades ago, two Chicago street gangs merged to form what would ultimately be known as the Gangster Disciples, which was led by Larry Hoover until his 1973 conviction for ordering a double murder. From his prison cell, Hoover masterminded a restructuring of the gang by instituting two boards: an incarcerated board for gang leaders in prison, and a board of leaders outside prison to run the gang's $100 million per year drug enterprise. Hoover's jailhouse reform resulted in a system to collect proceeds from drug sales by requiring that a tax be paid to the Gangster Disciples for drugs sold by individuals not associated with the gang, and that severe punishment be administered on other gangs that attempted to sell drugs in territories controlled by the Gangster Disciples. In 1990, Shell, already a board member on the outside, was elevated to second-in-command and in charge of the gang's street-level drug sales. Ironically, about the time of Shell's elevation, he and Irwin began living together.

However, it was Hoover's cunning and proficient organizational skills that posed a clear threat to the people of Chicago as well as a challenge to the law enforcement community and, in a very real sense, the city's political structure. For example, Hoover was aware that his telephone conversations from prison were subject to being intercepted; therefore, when he discussed the gang's criminal activities, he insisted that members of the gang visit the prison for face-to-face discussions. However, in 1993, the government wised up and distributed visitor badges equipped with transmitters to monitor Hoover's instruction to gang underlings. The badges were eventually discovered.

During 1993, the newly promoted Shell visited Hoover in prison, telling him that he planned to purchase a restaurant called June's Shrimp on the Nine. Thinking that the $15,000 purchase was a sound investment, and perhaps thinking futuristically, Hoover encouraged other gang members to invest in real estate. Shell's idea was to turn the restaurant over to his mother. Shell informed Hoover that Irwin would maintain the books for the restaurant and, because of her standing as a Chicago police officer, could equip the restaurant with guns. However, the discussion with Hoover does not indicate that Irwin was onboard or even aware of Shell's description of her role; and though the restaurant was purchased with drug proceeds, Shell's plan appears to indicate that it would operate as a lawful small business.

In the end, it was Irwin and not Shell who purchased the restaurant. In late 1993, Irwin, along with Shell, met with the seller's attorney to execute the contract of sale, purchasing the restaurant for $13,500, with a check drawn on Irwin's account for $8,000, a contract and a promissory note for the remaining $5,550 was executed by the gang crimes police officer. While the government alleged that the funds for purchasing the restaurant actually came from illegal proceeds provided by Shell, and that Irwin was acting as a legitimate front for the gang, at trial the prosecution did not present proof that this was the arrangement. Following the purchase, Irwin completed the necessary filings with the state of Illinois to run the restaurant through a corporate entity.

Irwin's appeal indicates that after the restaurant deal was finalized, a court order was approved to monitor the restaurant's phone. It is a matter of record that Irwin worked at the restaurant performing duties that any restaurant owner would be expected to do, such as ordering supplies and taking orders from customers. It is also true that Shell spent time working at the restaurant. In one recorded conversation with another gang leader, Shell said that he was busy cooking for a funeral that the restaurant was catering. Shell and others often used the restaurant's phone to talk with coconspirators. Shell issued orders over this phone, even once notifying two gang governors that their territories had been increased. And the phone was regularly used to instruct members to get the "weekly" and "political" in, although there is no evidence that the money was collected at the restaurant.

In the summer of 1994, Irwin's relationship with Shell took a turn for the worse when she telephoned the restaurant and spoke with Shell, calling him a liar and a sneak. Appearing overwhelmed by what was going on, Irwin threatened to send police officers to the restaurant, saying, "And I'm gonna tell you somethin else, those punks up there in that restaurant, you don't get 'em from the fuck out there, I'm gonna send the police up there from now on, and I mean that, I'm lettin you know." When Shell called her back, Irwin again threatened him, saying that, "I want your shit out of my house. I want them punks out of that restaurant, or I'm gone call the motherfucker police, or you get it out of my name."[7]

While Irwin and Shell sorted things out, the prosecution was busy putting together charges of conspiracy; and on August 31, 1995, three separate indictments charging 39 leaders of the Gangster Disciples and others with conspiracy to sell narcotics were handed down. One of the indictments charged Irwin along with nine codefendants. The indictments covering several criminal counts named Irwin in only the first, charging her with conspiracy in violation of 21 U.S.C. section 846. The government's charge that Irwin was an object of the conspiracy with the intent to distribute cocaine, crack cocaine, heroin, and marijuana was perceived as a success by some; yet to others, it was viewed as a blatant, politically driven overreach.

On January 29, 1996, Irwin along with her codefendants went to trial. However, in trying Irwin, the government did not attempt to demonstrate that she had actually joined the conspiracy, but instead asserted that she had aided and abetted the operation. It was clear that the intention was to convict the former police officer of a felonious act. To what can only be described as shock and dismay of those who knew the former gang crimes officer, the government's strategy worked, and the district court imposed a sentence of 151 months in federal prison, also fining Irwin $5,000.

Irwin appealed in a timely manner by challenging the district court's conviction based on a general argument and a more specific one, contending that:

> One cannot be liable for aiding and abetting a conspiracy where one has given aid to conspirators after the conspiratorial agreement is complete. To address this argument, we must interpret the federal statute that creates aider and abettor liability, 18 U.S.C. sec. 2(a), and the statute covering the substantive offense that Irwin was convicted of aiding and abetting, 21 U.S.C. sec. 846. We address these questions of law de novo. Irwin's more specific argument is that even if such liability is possible, insufficient evidence supports her conviction. When we address this second question we look at the evidence in the light most favorable to the government and ask whether "any rational trier of fact could have found the essential elements of the crime beyond a reasonable doubt."

The specificity of Irwin's conviction on the premise that she aided and abetted a conspiracy according to federal criminal code used in prosecuting her, identifies principals and accessories as two categories of offenders, defining the principal as:

> "Whoever commits an offense against the United States or aids, abets, counsels, commands, induces or procures its commission, is punishable as a principal." 18 U.S.C. sec. 2(a); see also Wright v. United States, 139 F.3d 551, 552 (7th Cir. 1998) ("The essence of

aider and abettor liability is that a person is punished as a principal even though he did not commit the actual elements of the crime."); United States v. Petty, 132 F.3d 373, 377 (7th Cir. 1998) ("In a sense, the essential elements of aiding and abetting serve as a substitute for the defendant's actual physical participation in the crime."). On the other hand, an accessory after the fact, one who aids after the crime has been committed, is liable for only half the maximum penalty to which the principal he assisted would be liable, to a maximum of 15 years. (18 U.S.C. sec. 3).

For over a century, the federal statute applicable to punishing an aider and abettor as a principal has been based on a test that weighs three elements: knowledge of the illegal activity that is being aided and abetted, a desire to help that activity succeed, and some act of helping. The prevailing statute does not delineate aiding and abetting, leaving it to the courts. A determination must be made regarding whether the aider is in any way linked to the scheme, participates in a way to help achieve it, and through their action strives to carry out the venture. As it relates to Irwin's appeal, the court indicated that it would uphold her conviction if it was shown that she was aware of the cocaine distribution conspiracy, meant to promote its success, and was a factor in at least one act of being in accord with the plot. The statute used during the original conviction of Irwin indicates that, "Any person who attempts or conspires to commit any offense defined in this subchapter shall be subject to the same penalties as those prescribed for the offense, the commission of which was the object of the attempt or conspiracy."[8] In what seems an ambiguous standard to convict Irwin—or anyone else, for that matter—under the statute, it is not necessary to prove that she or a coconspirator committed an explicit act to advance the conspiracy. The reason is that, according to the statute, consenting to commit a single substantive offense covered in the statute is considered to be the crime. The court agreed that Irwin's argument that one who assists after the agreement is made is an accessory after the fact has logic. However, in rejecting the argument, the court said that to argue that one is punished for their thoughts ignores the element of criminal accountability, which is the illegal act or omission that consists of the physical components of a criminal act.

What is particularly striking about Irwin's appeal is the straightforward acknowledgment in asking that the court reverse *United States v. Galiffa,* 734 F.2d 306 (7th Cir. 1984), in which the court disallowed the same argument. The defendant contended in *Galiffa* that "because a conspiracy is an agreement to commit an unlawful act, one can only aid and abet a conspiracy by aiding the formation of the agreement, such as bringing the parties together." However, the court held that "this interpretation of the conspiracy statute is too restrictive ... [A] person can be guilty of aiding and abetting a conspiracy when the person commits an act designed to further the conspiracy."[9]

Ironically, the court did not rebut the degree of logic as it relates to Irwin's contention that to regard the crime of conspiracy as having been committed when the pact is made, directly conflicts with the treatment of an individual who assists after the agreement is made, as an aider and abettor, rather than accessory after the fact. However, in defending its decision, the court indicated that it often regards a conspiracy as an ongoing undertaking, analyzing it based on the object of the conspiracy, goal, or purpose. Moreover, that the definition of the offense itself, as detailed in Section 846, makes the conspiracy's object critical; and includes only those conspiracies whose object purpose is to violate specific federal drug laws. However, the threshold for the government is to prove that those charged with participating in the conspiracy not only knew about it, but also were willing to participate in the illegal activity. Moreover, in order for a defendant to claim that they withdrew from participation in the conspiracy, they must totally withdraw as well as take steps to negate the purpose of the conspiracy and nefarious acts associated with it.

Irwin's defense and the court's decision therefore begs the question of what the guidelines are for proving involvement in a conspiracy. For the purposes of Irwin's case, *United States v. Jarrett*, 133 F.3d 519, 533 (7th Cir. 1998), was cited. It indicates that, "In order to prove that [the defendants] were members of the charged conspiracy, the Government was required to demonstrate that they knew of the conspiracy and that they intended to join and associate themselves with the conspiracy's criminal purposes." In addition, the court also cites the coconspirator exception to the hearsay rule, *Fed. R.Evid.* 801(d)(2)(E). The court also referred to statements made "during the course and in furtherance of the conspiracy," and by exampling *Townsend*, 924 F.2d at 1388–89, the court indicated that "a conspirator is liable for the substantive crimes of his coconspirators, again, when those crimes are committed in furtherance of the conspiracy."[10]

In what seems an effort to cover all its bases, the court found that there was no inconsistency in its conclusion that Irwin could be found guilty of aiding and abetting the crime of conspiracy through her action, advancing the attainment of the conspiracy's object, goal, or purpose. The court explained its ruling by saying that:

"This is so because when in assessing liability for the conspirators themselves these terms guide our analysis. The difference between an aider and abettor and an accomplice after the fact is not judged simply by asking whether the one aided could, when the aid is given, already be found guilty of the crime. Accessories after the fact are ones who give aid after the criminal endeavor has ended to keep the one aided from being caught or punished." In United States v. Osborn, 120 F.3d 59, 63 (7th Cir. 1997) (elements of accessory after the fact are underlying crimes committed by someone other than the defendant, knowledge of crime, and "assistance by the defendant in order to prevent the apprehension, trial or punishment of the offender") (quoting United States v. Lepanto, 817 F.2d 1463, 1467 (10th Cir. 1987)). Conspiracies can continue for a long time. (The conspiracy in this case lasted more than 20 years.) As we noted in Galiffa, if we accepted Irwin's argument, we would create a loophole for persons who do not join the conspiracy but who render valuable assistance that furthers its goals. 734 F.2d at 310. We see no reason to overrule our prior law.[11]

The court went on to point to what it termed as an abundance of evidence to validate Irwin's conviction, by examining the second question of whether the government had offered adequate proof to uphold the conviction. In doing so, it closely considered the requirements necessary to prove aider-and-abettor liability, indicating that it had to prove the existence of three elements: knowledge of the crime, a desire or intent to make the crime succeed, and at least one act of affirmative assistance. Irwin did not dispute that she was aware of the conspiracy and of Shell's participation in it, but instead concentrated her arguments on the desire and intent to make the crime succeed. However, the court indicated that in this case, like many others, the elements are joined. While the government possessed no direct evidence that she intended to further the conspiracy, Irwin's actions had to be related to circumstantial evidence. The court, by referencing United States v. Gabriel, 810 F.2d 627, 636 (7th Cir. 1987) asserted that:

("Proof of this criminal intent may be inferred from the surrounding circumstances."); United States v. Boykins, 9 F.3d 1278, 1284 (7th Cir. 1993) (same). Such circumstantial evidence can include evidence that the defendant had a motive to further the crime such as the defendant having a pecuniary stake in the success of the crime, see, e.g., Giovannetti, 919 F.2d at 1227; Blankenship, 970 F.2d at

286 (discussing pecuniary stake in differentiating one-time supplier from co-conspirator), or the defendant having a personal motive such as his relationship to one of the principals, see Pearson, 113 F.3d at 762 (defendant had father-and-son-like relationship with principal). And the aid that the defendant gave to the criminal enterprise can be used to support the inference that the defendant by giving the aid intended to further the crime; the law imputes to a defendant the intent to do that which is the natural consequence of his knowing acts. See Jacks v. Duckworth, 651 F.2d 480, 486 (7th Cir. 1981) (no error in instructing jury that everyone is presumed to intend the natural consequences of his voluntary acts); United States v. Machi, 811 F.2d 991, 998 (7th Cir. 1987) (intent to obstruct justice could be proved by evidence that such obstruction was natural consequence of defendant's acts); Trzcinski v. American Casualty Co., 953 F.2d 307, 313 (7th Cir. 1992) ("the law presumes 'every man to intend the natural consequences of his acts'") (quoting Tenore v. American and Foreign Insurance Co., 256 F.2d 791, 794-95 (7th Cir. 1958)). So when a defendant knowingly renders aid to a criminal endeavor and the natural consequence of such aid is to further the crime and help it succeed, the jury is entitled to infer that the defendant intended by his assistance to further the crime. In a case such as this where the evidence of the defendant's intent must be inferred from the aid given, the second and third elements really merge and our review focuses on whether the aid given was sufficient to support the inference of intent to further the crime.[12]

The court said that because the aid that a defendant gives frequently fulfills two purposes, as direct evidence of affirmative assistance and circumstantial evidence of intent. This suggests that moderating the analysis of aider and abettor and focusing specifically on the amount of assistance known to have been provided is in keeping with determining whether the assistance was "deliberate and material." The court concluded that:

But what if he merely rendered assistance, without being compensated or otherwise identifying with the goals of the principal? We do not think it should make a difference, provided the assistance is deliberate and material. One who, knowing the criminal nature of another's act, deliberately renders what he knows to be active aid in the carrying out of the act is, we think, an aider and abettor even if there is no evidence that he wants the acts to succeed—even if he is merely acting in the spirit of mischief. The law rarely has regard for underlying motives.[13]

The court held that in cases such as Irwin's, a requirement of material assistance would not matter, adding that the prospect of a defendant intentionally providing material assistance, though there is no indication of a desire for the criminal act to be successful, is unlikely. The court's ironclad defense of the original verdict effactually sealed Irwin's fate in the eyes of the court as an aider and abettor, regardless of whether she actively participated or had knowledge of the criminal enterprise, and did nothing to prevent it.

So, in spite of Irwin's vigorous and reasonable argument that the government offered no evidence to show that she had a financial interest in the success of the illegal drug enterprise, the court considered it as insignificant, and that Irwin's motivation for rendering aid had no bearing. In explaining, the court offered that the significance of the defendant's motivation to assist in a conspiracy does not matter, but that the defendant knew that there was an illegal conspiracy underway and acquiesced to assist, making the success of the conspiracy more likely. As it relates to the relationship between Shell and Irwin, suggestions offered to explain any level whatsoever of involvement were deemed irrelevant. The court achieved this by stating that:

Whatever motive or combination of motives inspired her actions, the significant question is whether she knew of the crime and by her actions intended to further it; and her intent can be inferred from the natural consequences of her knowing acts. On the other hand, the government's arguments seem to suggest, although they recognize the intent element, that knowledge of the crime and any assistance is sufficient to prove aiding and abetting, even if there is no other evidence of intent and the assistance is not material. None of our prior cases has suggested this is the appropriate test.

Irwin asked the court to analyze and determine if the assistance she gave was "substantial," as per the language of 15 U.S.C. section 78t(f) (as it relates to aiders and abettors of securities crimes). The request leads to the question of whether the outcome of her actions to assist aided in making the crime more likely to succeed. The court's answer was that it did, and that unlike the example of the store clerk who knowingly sells a dress to a prostitute that will be used in furtherance of her trade, and in doing so is offering affirmative assistance, the aid that is offered by the clerk is considered trivial and too far removed from the actual criminal act of the prostitute to infer criminal intent. In Irwin's case, the challenge was to examine the evidence and determine whether a jury of her peers could beyond a reasonable doubt find her guilty of aiding and abetting a criminal conspiracy. The government argued that Irwin advanced the conspiracy in three ways, saying that: "She permitted Shell to use a charge card on her account; she assisted Shell in renting cars so that he could visit Hoover in prison; and she was involved in purchasing and running June's Shrimp on the Nine." In Irwin's effort to successfully appeal the conviction, and the court's all-out effort to uphold it, here are three key details that demonstrate the distance between someone that had been a valued member of law enforcement, and a person that the criminal justice system now seemed to go out of its way to imprison and to make an example of.

1. SHELL'S USE OF IRWIN'S CHARGE CARD

Irwin had an American Express account on which Shell was a cardholder —that is, Shell had a card with his name on it, but purchases made with his card were billed to Irwin's account. The record shows that over about two years, Shell made about $7,000 in purchases with this card. The government asserts that this evidence shows Irwin intended to further the conspiracy because she provided Shell with a charge card "through which he could spend his ill-gotten gains." Thus, the government argues, Irwin's providing Shell the charge card was like the defendant in *Griffin* (84 F.3d at 929), an attorney found to be an aider and abettor of a conspiracy because he aided conspirators in laundering their drug money after the conspiracy was formed. However, the comparison exaggerates the credit card's impact. Even if Shell's use of this card to make purchases provided some assistance to the conspiracy—an inference of which we are uncertain is supported by the record—it was of such trivial assistance that it cannot support the inference that Irwin intended by it to further the conspiracy's success. Importantly, Shell's use of the charge card did not hide his identity because the card was issued in his name. In fact his use of the card created a paper trail leading to him. These purchases took place over two years, so they averaged less than $300 per month, a trivial amount compared to the scope of this conspiracy. (Whereas it is estimated that the gains from members of the Gangster Disciples who would "donate" their profits from drug sales one day each week to supervisory levels of the gang, known as "nation work" and "one-day-a-week," netted Hoover $200,000 to $300,000 per week.) Whatever assistance this might have been, $7,000 in two years is—standing alone—too insignificant to support the inference that with such aid, Irwin intended to further the conspiracy's success. Although use of the card indicated a close relationship between Irwin and Shell, the natural consequence of Irwin letting Shell use the card is not that the conspiracy would be more likely to succeed, even if letting him use the card could be seen as an affirmative act of assistance.

2. IRWIN'S RENTING A CAR FOR SHELL

The government also contends that Irwin aided and abetted the conspiracy when she rented a car for Shell to use when visiting Hoover in prison. The thrust of the government's theory on appeal is that the rental car was essential because it disguised Shell's identity when he visited Hoover. As a prior convicted felon, Shell would not have been permitted to visit Hoover without obtaining a waiver from prison officials, so Shell used an alias. The government argued that by providing a rental car for Shell, Irwin assisted Shell in maintaining his alias, because if the prison officials were to check the license plate of the car, it would come back as belonging to the rental agency and not Shell. Irwin does not dispute that she knew Shell was visiting Hoover and that he was using an alias to do so. The question is whether the aid of renting a car for Shell sufficiently supports the inference of intent to further the conspiracy. It falls short because of a gap in the government's evidence.

The initial difficulty with the government's theory is that it depends on there being something in the record supporting the inference that Shell's motive—at least in part—in using the rental car was to hide his identity from the prison officials, a proposition for which there is no support in the record. There is no direct evidence of Shell's motive in renting the car, nor is there circumstantial evidence to show a motive that supports the government's theory. The government presented evidence that the prison officials checked identification when someone came to visit Vienna, and that the prison guards would input the visitor's name into a computer. But the government did not offer any evidence regarding prison officials checking license plates. Nor did the government offer evidence that had the license plates been checked, Shell's identity would not have been known, for he sometimes rented cars in his own name or was identified as an authorized driver, and only once used an alias in connection with renting a car. All this record shows is that on several occasions, Irwin rented a car and listed Shell as a driver. And on more than one occasion, she got a police discount from the rental company, 15 percent in one case. This financial aid is insufficient to support the inference of intent to further the conspiracy. Without evidence of the license plate inspection, the slight savings on the cost of the rental car is inconsequential. Irwin's getting a discount for Shell was no real assistance. A 15 percent discount on a car rental was effectively meaningless to the success of a conspiracy this big. (He usually rented a high-cost car anyway.) Although it would be of some measurable aid to the organization, it could not reasonably be said to "materially" or "substantially" further its goals. Furthermore, even if Shell had thought a rental car was essential to facilitate his visits to Hoover, by disguising his identity or otherwise, the government presented no evidence that it would have been more difficult for Shell to have obtained a rental car without Irwin, that Irwin's renting the car for him was also essential. Like the evidence of Shell's use of Irwin's credit card, Irwin's renting the car for Shell simply cannot, by itself, support the inference of intent. Because of Irwin's involvement with the restaurant (see below), we need not decide whether the credit card use and car rental could support that inference when combined with other evidence.

3. IRWIN'S INVOLVEMENT WITH THE RESTAURANT

We now turn to the more substantial evidence of Irwin's aid to the conspiracy: her involvement with June's Shrimp on the Nine. Although the government describes the restaurant as a "nerve center" for the conspiracy, that characterization magnifies the facts. The restaurant was not the only place, or even the main place, where the conspirators met. The record showed that Shell held meetings at another restaurant in the neighborhood, and he held meetings and collected payments at a place called the Criss Cross Lounge. Shell used the phone at June's Shrimp on the Nine to instruct coconspirators to get their payments to him, but the record does not show that these payments were delivered to him at that restaurant. Even though the restaurant was not a so-called "nerve center," it did play a significant role in the conspiracy. The government monitored thousands of gang-related calls coming in and going out. And members of the conspiracy, including some of its top leaders, were frequently at the restaurant. The critical question here, of course, is not whether the restaurant provided aid to the conspiracy, but whether Irwin's acts vis-à-vis the restaurant sufficiently support the inference of intent to benefit the conspiracy. They do.

Irwin furthered the conspiracy's goals in several ways. She acted as the nominal owner of the restaurant, which distanced the restaurant from Shell and the other members of the gang. While Irwin had a legitimate job that could explain how she got the money to purchase the restaurant, Shell was collecting public assistance and had testified in a paternity suit against him that he had no source of income, so his buying a restaurant for $13,500 would be suspicious. Moreover, Irwin did more than simply let Shell put her name on the papers; she conducted the transaction herself, signing the purchase contract and promissory note. And Irwin went further, using the services of an attorney to create a corporation that she maintained for two years by filing the appropriate forms with the state and paying the necessary fees. Irwin also worked in the restaurant to maintain the appearance, at least, that it was a legitimate business. And importantly, Irwin at least once asserted some control over the gang's activities in the restaurant in an effort to maintain that appearance of legitimacy. She called the restaurant and dictated that one of the gang, Garnett, should not be permitted to use the phone because he talked too much. She said, "And I don't want him talking to anybody about anything. The only thing he's supposed to do is look out for you." Irwin said that she had told Shell about her decision. She explained, "Cuz see I have faith in you Marty, I don't have faith in in, in Garnett and them [others]. ... I don't know nothin' about them." This evidence permitted the inference that Irwin was assisting Shell in maintaining a clubhouse or meeting place for the gang and providing it with a veneer of legitimacy. The natural consequence of these acts is that the conspiracy would be more likely to succeed, so these acts at least sufficiently support the inference of intent. And so, because she concedes knowledge, her conviction was supported by sufficient evidence.

When Irwin raised what would be her final point of argument, that she was being unfairly convicted because she was a police officer, and that her conviction was not based on tangible evidence, the court rejected it in a statement that bordered on petty: "We agree that the government and its witnesses made frequent reference to her being a police officer, but she seems not to have objected to this evidence below nor on appeal does she claim error in its admission. We therefore have no occasion to determine whether its admission was correct."[14] In the end, the court affirmed Irwin's conviction.

Taking into account what was happening in Chicago during the 1990s, and for that matter across the country, as law enforcement agencies fortified their stance against gangbangers and drugs, Irwin's conviction stands as an example of the political nature of our criminal justice system. This is especially relevant in light of the 2010 conviction of former CPD police commander Jon Burge and the subsequent release from prison of scores of criminal suspects that were wrongfully arrested by Burge's rogue gang of police officers, and it strengthens the case for those who believe there was an ulterior motive in prosecuting Irwin. If nothing else, Burge's conviction points up the stark irony in the criminal justice system, one that contributes to unlawful arrests, torture-induced confessions, and over-the-top police misconduct, while seeming to go out of its way to build a case and to aggressively prosecute another former officer. While the conviction of Burge is something that continues to taint the reputation of Chicago's law enforcement community, Irwin's trial, conviction, and appeal are, except for those with a personal connection or that benefitted from it, all but forgotten.

The sticking point for many is that they find it unfathomable that the former six-term mayor Richard M. Daley, who as state's attorney, serving almost a decade at the helm of Cook County law enforcement, knew nothing about the scores of individuals wrongly arrested, tortured and prosecuted by Burge. Therefore, speculation continues that Daley and his underlings must have known about the outrageous behavior that has resulted in the release of scores of innocent individuals who were wrongly imprisoned, and the millions of taxpayer dollars paid to settle with those affected by the shameful action.

Aside from the astounding financial liability is the impact of police wrongdoing and corruption on the relationship between the people in the neighborhoods and upstanding police officers who patrol those neighborhoods. Whether former CPD officer Irwin was, for political reasons singled out for severe prosecution in order to divert attention from the reprehensible actions of former CPD commander Jon Burge, remains open to speculation.

NOTES

1. Peter Ustinov, quoted in http://thinkexist.com/quotation/corruption_is_nature-s_way_of_restoring_our_faith/218508.html   (accessed October 30, 2014).

2. Aurora, Illinois, police officer Aaron Jones, interview by author, 2014.

3. William Recktenwald and Colin McMahon, "Deadly End to Deadly Year," *Chicago Tribune*, January 1, 1993, http://articles.chicagotribune.com/1993-01-01/news/9303175195_1_murder-rate-deadly-year-gunshot (accessed February 7, 2014).

4. Judy Pasternak, "U.S. Moves to Crack Powerful Chicago Gang," *Los Angeles Times*, September 1, 1995, http://articles.latimes.com/1995-09-01/news/mn-41129_1_chicago-s-gangster-disciples (accessed April 2, 2014).

5. Matt O'Connor, *Chicago Tribune*, February 28, 1996.

6. Appeal from the United States District Court for the Northern District of Illinois, Eastern Division, No. 95 CR 509—Paul E. Plunkett, Judge, argued January 21, 1998, decided July 1, 1998.

7. *United States v. Irwin*, http://caselaw.findlaw.com/us-7th-circuit/1365088.html (accessed July 13, 2014).

8. http://openjurist.org/149/f3d/565/united-states-v-irwin (accessed July 13, 2014).

9. *United States v. Irwin*.

10. Ibid.

11. http://njlaw.rutgers.edu/collections/resource.org/fed_reporter/F3/149/149.F3d.565.html (accessed October 30, 2014).

12. Ibid.

13. https://casetext.com/case/united-states-v-irwin-11 (accessed October 31, 2013).

14. Ibid.

8

❖

Technology and the Police

"The law of unintended consequences governs all technological revolutions."[1]

POLICING TECHNOLOGY HISTORY

The crime-fighting technology available during the 1940s and 1950s would have marveled the law enforcement professionals of the 1900s. Just think, what a difference it would have made if the innovations that were available to Sergeant Joe Friday (a character from the 1950s law enforcement television series *Dragnet*), had existed a half-century earlier. One of the few techniques still in use by modern-day police officers from the inception of American law enforcement is good, old-fashioned, door-to-door police work, and in the arsenal of contemporary policing, it too is fading fast.

Modern-day law enforcement has at its disposal state-of-the art dispatch centers, surveillance pods, personal computers, forensics, advanced weaponry, the FBI's National Crime Information Center's (NCIC) database, and, for almost three decades, deoxyribonucleic acid (DNA), which is increasingly more relied on than fingerprinting and the polygraph. On the horizon are drones and other innovations that, in the near future, will assist police officers in performing their duties and virtually make extinct shoe-leather policing techniques. Still, some citizens clamor for boots on the ground in high-crime areas and believe that the deployment of officers in crime-ridden areas is an effective supplement to the cutting-edge crime-fighting technology available to contemporary law enforcement agencies.

The drive and expansion of law enforcement's technological resources, its know-how and techniques from primitive beginnings until now, result from the ongoing effort to counter the cunning and dastardly deeds of individuals and groups that are hell-bent on committing crimes against society. An examination of the history of law enforcement's crime-fighting technology and its inextricable link to the masterminds of criminal enterprise illustrates the ingenuity that has been brought to bear in the struggle to keep up and to defend against crime. However, technological advancement is a double-edged sword not only to law enforcement organizations, but also to the individuals who seek to perpetrate criminal acts. In addition, as police find new ways to use the technologies to monitor the urban landscape, maintain a digital record of crimes in progress, identify criminal suspects, and conduct interrogations, the evidence is obtainable to the prosecution and defense. It can be used to scrutinize the actions of police officers by defense attorneys who dissect every aspect of the information in an attempt to create reasonable doubt, or to demonstrate overzealousness, excessive force, or out-and-out police misconduct.

Another outcome can be an overreliance on technology by law enforcement to prove guilt. For example, one might deduce desperation, arrogance, or laziness on the part of law enforcement officials that utilized the digitally recorded, violent-laden lyrics of rap artist Vonte Skinner to convict him of attempted murder in 2008. Subsequently, Justice Jaynee LaVecchia of the Supreme Court of New Jersey rendered the opinion that "[o]ne would not presume that Bob Marley, who wrote the well-known song 'I Shot the Sheriff,' actually shot a sheriff, or that Edgar Allan Poe buried a man beneath his floorboards, as depicted in his short story 'The Tell-Tale Heart,' simply because of their respective artistic endeavors on those subjects. [Skinner's] lyrics should receive no different treatment."[2]

Some view the ratification of the Fourth Amendment of the U.S. Constitution in 1791, and the legislative history leading to the Federal Communications Act of 1934, as setting the parameters for wiretapping and making surveillance as the foundation of our criminal justice system, and the catalyst for the crime-fighting ingenuity to come. For example, according to a 2001 report titled *Internet Wiretapping and Carnivore*, the invention of the telegraph in 1844 resulted in the immediate use of wiretapping as a crime-fighting tool. Later inventions like the telephone opened the door for law enforcement to discover innovative ways for the use of wiretapping and other methods of surveillance in its crime-fighting efforts.

Great Britain is credited with being the first country to launch a national emergency telephone number. However, it is debatable if the modern-day evolution of technological advancement started with the implementation of our 911 emergency telephone system in 1968 in the town of Haleyville, Alabama. There are several law enforcement developments that are considered key in making technology a resource relied on by law enforcement organizations. For example, according to the Erie County, Pennsylvania, Public Department of Safety: "In November of 1967, the FCC met with AT&T officials to determine a national emergency number that could be implemented quickly. By early the next year, AT&T announced that they had decided on 911 as the best combination for the emergency number. It was easy to remember and had never been used as an area or service code. Telephone company equipment could be easily adjusted to accept the number."[3]

In detailing the basis and history of America's emergency number, the National Emergency Number Association (NENA) indicates the occurrence of the following as key events related to its implementation:

- In the United States, the first catalyst for a nationwide emergency telephone number was in 1957, when the National Association of Fire Chiefs recommended use of a single number for reporting fires.
- In 1967, the President's Commission on Law Enforcement and Administration of Justice recommended that a "single number should be established" nationwide for reporting emergency situations. The use of different telephone numbers for each type of emergency was determined to be contrary to the purpose of a single, universal number.

The effort to establish a national emergency number eventually garnered the support of federal agencies and movement to implement the system. However, it would require a directive from the President's Commission on Civil Disorders to the Federal Communications Commission (FCC) to remove any obstacles and to initiate the system. These are believed to be the key decisions leading to the establishment of the nation's emergency telephone number:

- The code 911 was chosen because it best fit the needs of all parties involved. First, and most importantly, it met public requirements because it is brief, easily remembered, and can be dialed quickly. Second, because it is a unique number, never having been authorized as an office code, area code, or service code, it best met the long-range numbering plans and switching configurations of the telephone industry.

- Congress backed AT&T's proposal and passed legislation allowing use of only the numbers 911 when creating a single emergency-calling service, thereby making 911 a standard emergency number nationwide. A Bell System policy was established to absorb the cost of central office modifications and any additions necessary to accommodate the 911 code as part of the general rate base.
- With Enhanced 911, or E911, local PSAPs are responsible for paying network trunking costs according to tariffed rates, and for purchasing telephone-answering equipment from the vendor of their choice.
- On February 16, 1968, Senator Rankin Fite completed the first 911 call made in the United States in Haleyville, Alabama. The serving telephone company was then Alabama Telephone Company. This Haleyville 911 system is still in operation today.
- In March 1973, the White House's Office of Telecommunications issued a national policy that recognized the benefits of 911, encouraged the nationwide adoption of 911, and provided for the establishment of a Federal Information Center to assist units of government in planning and implementation.[4]

According to About.com Inventors, in the 1970s, the computerization of law enforcement agencies known as Computer Assisted Dispatch (CAD) began the centralization of integrated dispatching of police, fire, and medical services for large metropolitan areas. In 1972, the National Institute of Justice initiated a project that led to the use of Kevlar as a protective body armor to help protect police officers. It is credited with saving the lives of thousands of law enforcement personnel. The 1970s also introduced the use of night vision gear and the fingerprint identification system.

The key 1980 advancements in law enforcement efforts brought, for example, improvements to the 911 system. The enhancements allowed police dispatchers to determine the originating access addresses and telephone number of 911 calls. A couple of years later, Oleoresin Capsicum (OC) pepper spray, which is synthesized from capsaicin, was widely used by police officers in lieu of physical force.

The 1990s brought more technological advances as computers became more commonly used by law enforcement agencies and prominently used in police squad cars. Computerization aided in the analysis of crime data as well as the strategic utilization of law enforcement personnel. In 1996, the reliability of DNA evidence received the support of the National

Academy of Sciences, changing law enforcement organizations and the entire American justice system.

In a 2004 issue of the *Police Chief*, a monthly magazine, Paul D. Schultz, chief of police of Lafayette, Colorado, elaborated on the technologies available to police officers a decade ago. Schultz's references to things like crime lights, in-car camera systems, photo enforcement systems, Graffiti cameras, thermal imaging, improved radios, and Automatic License Plate Recognition, all worthy of praise, have been greatly improved upon, or entirely replaced by newer technologies.

The know-how available to police today showcases the remarkable advancements made since Chief Schultz's description of the state-of-the-art equipment that existed little more than a decade ago. For example, improvements to the surveillance equipment in police squad cars were introduced in 2013 Ford Police Interceptors. According to Security Technology News reporter Emma Murphy, "The new surveillance technology will use the existing Ford driver-assist equipment comprising of a backup camera, cross-traffic alert and reverse park assist, used previously as parking tools, to give the police officers an increased awareness of their situation and provide an added defense from would-be attackers."[5]

Who knew only several decades ago that today, one of the most urgent and complex challenges for federal, state, and local law enforcement agencies would be related to the relatively recent threat of cybercrime. The simplified description of cybercrime is an illegal activity that uses a computer to perpetrate criminal acts. However, according to the Offices of the United States Attorneys, "Cybercrime is one of the greatest threats facing our country, and has enormous implications for our national security, economic prosperity, and public safety. Attorney General Eric Holder has made it one of the Department of Justice's top priorities. The range of threats and the challenges they present for law enforcement expand just as rapidly as technology evolves."[6]

Cybercrimes are perpetrated by individuals who spread computer viruses and participate in identity theft, computer hacking, the theft of governmental and intellectual property, terrorism, cyberbullying, and stalking. The exponential expansion of cybercrime threatens individuals, financial institutions, public utilities, and American industry.

The FBI and other law enforcement agencies continue to utilize what is available to them to counter the escalating victimization caused by cybercrime and its impact on the American population. However, as lawmakers and the courts deal with the effect of cybercrime, they must also contend with concerns raised by the ACLU about the government's use of advanced technology and its intrusion on individual liberties. Many agree with the ACLU's position that the tools and surveillance techniques used to eradicate all types of crime, including cybercrime, does not mean that individual rights should be trampled. It is believed that technologies like cybernetics, crime recreation, and drones are merely the first steps toward law enforcement's use of robocops to patrol American streets in self-driven squad cars, and that Hollywood scriptwriters several decades ago may have gotten this one right.

MODERN POLICE SURVEILLANCE TECHNIQUES

The Orwellian advances that affect almost every area of modern-day life are nothing short of astounding. We live in a world where, for better or worse, nothing is beyond belief. It's a world wherein the age-old question "What will they think of next?" has been changed to "Who will think of it first?"

Law enforcement agencies are no exception, and the effect of modern technology is having a dramatic influence on the entire criminal justice system. However, arguably, at the forefront is the deployment of the cutting-edge technology that law enforcement officials are using or planning to use as crime deterrents. For example, the fact that the United Kingdom's omnipresent closed-circuit television camera (CCTV) surveillance system, said to utilize 1.85 million cameras—or, to illustrate its personal effect, one CCTV for every 32 citizens of Great Britain—while incredible, is no longer shocking. The reality is that there are those that perceive the elaborate network of observation devices as performing a necessary function by helping to protect the public against crime and acts of terrorism, while others perceive the CCTV as an invasion of their individual liberties and privacy. Still, use of the cameras has by most been deemed a necessary tool to defend against crime, sabotage, and terrorist attacks. It should be noted that according to a 2013 United Kingdom *Telegraph* article, the number of CCTV cameras is said to be much higher. According to the story, "Britain has a CCTV camera for every 11 people, a security industry report disclosed, as privacy campaigners criticised the growth of the 'surveillance state.'"

The massive CCTV system that captures approximately 26 million images per day is comprised of cameras in public and private areas that are used for a variety of purposes that include combating crime, terrorism, and public safety. According to the *Christian Science Monitor*, "The civil rights group Liberty estimates that the average Londoner is captured on camera around 300 times a day while BBW claims Britain has 20 percent of the world's CCTV cameras and only 1 percent of the world's population."[7] In the United Kingdom *Telegraph* article, privacy campaign director Nick Pickles, who heads the Big Brother Watch, referred to the increasing use of CCTV in the UK as follows:

> This report is another stark reminder of how out of control our surveillance culture has become.
>
> With potentially more than five million CCTV cameras across country, including more than 300,000 cameras in schools, we are being monitored in a way that few people would recognise as a part of a healthy democratic society.
>
> This report should be a wake up call that in modern Britain there are people in positions of responsibility who seem to think '1984' was an instruction manual.[8]

The expansion of technology to improve public safety and secure public and private assets has created a boon in security and related industries. Innovators and manufacturers of security technology are under pressure to stay a step ahead by creating technology that will nullify or weaken attempts by those that would harm or wreak havoc on society. One aspect of the effort is the present and futuristic utilization of drones and other technological marvels to combat crime. The advances currently being discussed make the crime-fighting techniques depicted in the 2002 Steven Spielberg movie *Minority Report*, in which police are able to forecast and arrest individuals before they commit crimes, appear within reach, and their use in modern-day law enforcement efforts at hand. In fact, signs of it are seen in large police departments like LAPD, NYPD, and the CPD, where forecasting the occurrence of criminal acts within certain geographic areas is currently utilized. The all-important surveillance tools are key in the wide range of attempts to identify nefarious acts that target the innocent, before they occur. For instance, in Mexico, "Silent Angels" (deaf police officers), out of the public's view, watch over citizens helping to protect them against street crime and the roving offenders that prey upon the innocent.

In 2013, the American surveillance apparatus and the methods used by the National Security Agency (NSA) came under intense criticism when it was revealed that the NSA had listened to the telephone conversations of 35 world leaders. Among those targeted by the NSA for eavesdropping were some of America's top allies and heads of state, including Germany and France. According to news reports, revelations that the personal cell phone conversations of German chancellor Angela Merkel had been intercepted by the United States bought this terse response from the German leader: "Spying between friends is simply unacceptable ... We need trust between partners and such trust needs to be re-established." Implying that the allegations, if proven, would represent a severe breach of trust, Merkel emphasized that, "We are allies facing challenges together. But such an alliance can only be built on the basis of trust. I repeat that spying among friends is not at all acceptable against anyone and that goes for every citizen in Germany."[9] The international backlash and criticism related to the revelations, and the extent of U.S. surveillance used against foreign governments, said to be necessary by law enforcement and NSA officials, prompted immediate condemnation.

After learning of the U.S. surveillance, Germany and France called for talks related to the U.S. spying. Worldwide reaction and outrage related to the methods used to collect information prompted President Obama to announce reforms associated with U.S. surveillance targets and techniques. At the same time, the domestic surveillance issue is fervently debated, with some asserting that it violates the guaranteed protections of privacy and civil liberties. The fact that investigative agencies, with the backing of the federal government, are allowed to utilize third parties to secretly collect personal information about American citizens is chilling and, on a number of levels, extremely troubling. One reason for concern is that it represents an encroachment on rights guaranteed by the U.S. Constitution. Yet, what tends to stand out most is the NSA's startling acknowledgment by high-ranking law enforcement officials that this method of gathering intelligence is necessary.

Americans realize that the need for heightened surveillance was ushered in during the aftermath of the 9/11 terrorist attacks. Essentially unbridled, radical measures were deemed necessary and, for the most part, acceptable. There is little dispute that 9/11 was the watershed moment, marking the beginning of an intensified focus on defending the U.S. homeland against foreign and domestic threats of terrorism, and changing the threshold of what many Americans were willing to accept as the price for protecting the homeland. After the 9/11 attacks, across the country, local law enforcement agencies were viewed as a united force on the frontline, defending the American people. Frequently reminded of their responsibility to remain vigilant, the American public, armed with their cellphones, fortified the effort to protect against acts of terrorism. In addition to residential security cameras, businesses became crucial partners in augmenting what everyday citizens and law enforcement agencies were doing by monitoring and reporting suspicious activities.

It was widely agreed that if security improvements at the federal level were to be successful in keeping Americans out of harm's way, improving and expanding technology at the local law enforcement level was necessary. Initially, federal funding to local law enforcement organizations was specifically earmarked for technology aimed at assisting in defending against terror threats. However, police commands across the country in due course realized that the application of technology would be effective in fighting urban crime. Eventually, they were able to use federal funding to purchase advanced technology in their effort to deter street crime, battle gangs and drug distribution, and decrease violence. As crime rates soared in some U.S. urban centers, the term "domestic terrorism" was used to include gang members and thugs that prey on the innocent. With murder, assault, rape, and robbery on the rise, it became easier for police departments to justify the use of surveillance equipment, originally designated to monitor threats of foreign-borne terrorism; and the technology could also be used to defend against domestic crime, thus getting a bigger "bang for the buck," so to speak.

Fox News illustrated the important role that residential surveillance cameras can have on inner-city crime by helping to supplement the police technology and strategies that are sometimes simply not enough. In 2013, the news agency reported that the arrest of two men charged in the nationally covered story of the murder of Chicago high school honor student Hadiya Pendleton was due to a homeowner's effort to protect his home, by installing residential security cameras. The cameras, intended to record the image of anyone attempting to break into the residence, had captured the image of the two individuals that were eventually charged in the 15-year-old's murder.

As early as 2003, in the aftermath of 9/11, cities such as Chicago, Los Angeles, and New York were aided by funding from the Department of Homeland Security (DHS). Not long after, municipalities began deploying, as part of their crime-fighting arsenal, cameras commonly known as surveillance pods. The pods, strategically mounted above the urban streetscape throughout urban America, cast an eerie shadow as they scrutinize citizens and secure images of suspicious activities and individuals in the commission of criminal acts.

However, there was an immediate and robust criticism of the use of this technology by the ACLU and other civil rights organizations, which argued that the devices were an invasion of privacy and a violation of constitutional liberties. Some went as far as to assert that the explosion of surveillance equipment, said to aid in controlling and reducing criminal activity, was itself a criminal act. Moreover, there was concern that the increasing intrusiveness of the technology would eventually morph into the use of facial recognition and inevitably expand to the utilization of U.S. military drones for domestic purposes.

It appears that the predictions are not far off the mark if one considers that over a decade ago, police departments in major urban centers increased the use and effectiveness of surveillance pods by making it possible for officers to use laptop computers from their squad cars to observe, in real time, the streets that they patrol. In 2003, the *Christian Science Monitor* provided this spine-chilling description of the surveillance cameras that hover over Chicago's inner city: "The cameras in these 'surveillance pods' are encased in bullet-proof glass and can rotate 360 degrees, focus in on activity four blocks away, and see at night. They will be conspicuous, marked by a flashing blue light atop the pod, and police can take them down and move them to another hot spot within a couple of hours."[10]

Chicago Police superintendent McCarthy's expanding use of data-driven strategies, some say, incorporates the much-needed reliance on social media as a tool to predict an outbreak of crime before it occurs. In the minds of some, it helps to allay fear, yet it has also created anxiety for others. As 2013 came to a close, crime-reporting sources indicated that CPD technology-focused strategies, and McCarthy's decision to go forward despite public outcry, had been a factor in reducing the city's overall crime rate. According to the *Chicago Tribune*, when compared to 2011, a 5 percent decline in homicides was realized. The CPD reported 435 murders in 2011, 503 in 2012, and 415 in 2013. The report also revealed a decline in the number of shootings, sexual assaults, serious battery, burglaries, and vehicle theft. However, fast forward to the July 4, 2014, weekend, when 14 people were killed and more than 80 wounded by gun violence, and one wonders if the advancement in technology is making a difference.

It is obvious the utilization of technology played a role in the notable decrease in Chicago's crime rates during 2013. However, also factoring into the decline were management decisions and improvements, such as training and redeploying police officers, in addition to a significant increase in overtime costs to Chicago taxpayers to the tune of a whopping $53 million. In a city where homicides surged to 849 in 1990, it is more likely that a combination of policing strategies and technology, including the controversial use of cameras in high-crime areas, played a significant role in reducing crime.

In urban America, a combination of measures, including the deployment of surveillance cameras, new policing strategies, and advancements in crime-fighting technologies, are being touted as the source of a decline in crime statistics overall. For example, in major U.S. cities, the role of technology is seen as essential in the effort to defend against the threat of terrorist attacks, street gang violence, open-air drug dealing, and a relatively new crime phenomena known as the flash-mob. These sometimes violent criminal mobs are organized through the use of social media and generally for the purpose of wreaking havoc on individuals and businesses. In one example, a Brooklyn mall was trashed and looted by a flash-mob of what was estimated as 400 teenagers. Ratcheting fear, the *New York Post* reported: "The troublemakers looted and ransacked several stores as panicked shoppers ran for the exits and clerks scrambled to pull down metal gates."[11]

As useful as it is in fighting crime and deterring the criminal element, utilization of technology has had a multifaceted effect on the relationship between law enforcement and American society. The pros, cons, and effects of technology on society depend largely on one's perspective. For example, the individual's viewpoint can be affected by factors such as race, socioeconomics, political persuasion, and the much-less-talked-about social consciousness. For example, a person's opinion regarding the use of technology to fight inner-city crime can boil down to whether they reside in a community where surveillance devices are present and its people under constant monitoring by law enforcement. However, from the point of view of one who resides in a neighborhood where crime is low, the surveillance equipment might be perceived as something that will help keep criminal activity at bay and therefore prompt an entirely different reaction. Either way, there is a psychological element that the manufacturers of the cutting-edge technologies are successfully using to market security-related devices to law enforcement agencies.

Indeed, it is an eerie feeling to travel through crime-ridden communities and suddenly be struck by the realization that the residents of an entire neighborhood are under the watchful eye of law enforcement as they go about their daily lives. That this is a reality does not bode well that, anytime soon, we will see an improvement in the relationship between the law enforcement community and the minority and economically disadvantaged population that reside in urban centers throughout America. In fact, the irony is that the very technology that is used to keep the citizenry safe has in some instances widened the gulf. This is because the notion of an omnipresent police is for some unacceptable, not to mention the implication that it represents a violation of guaranteed civil liberties.

As indicated, the use of technology in crime-fighting efforts is of tremendous value to law enforcement organizations. However, the flipside
of advancements in surveillance technology is its accessibility and afford-
ability to the general population. For example, according to a 2013 study
by the Pew Research Center, from 2004 to 2013, cell phone ownership
in the United States grew to a whopping 91 percent of the adult population. Moreover, a survey conducted by Pew Internet revealed, "56% of
American adults have smartphones."[12] Equipped with state-of-the-art
high-resolution cameras and video- and audio-recording capability, the
devices have been used to capture, in real time, irrefutable evidence of
police brutality. In one example, a 2014 video recording captured a
NYPD police officer using an illegal chokehold to restrain Eric Garner,
an asthmatic, who later died, prompting a public outcry and calls for an
investigation. In speaking about the images of Garner being placed in a
chokehold, images that received national media coverage, Reverend Al
Sharpton said, "The chokehold is illegal. But even if you lost your training
memory, a man in your arm saying 'I can't breathe' . . . when does your
decency kick in?" Continuing, Sharpton asserted, "Let's not play games
with this one. You don't need no training to stop choking a man saying
'I can't breathe.' You don't need no cultural orientation to stop choking
a man saying 'I can't breathe.' You need to be prosecuted."[13]

The video images of the police action that Sharpton refers to is supported by many more examples of technology catching police officers in
the act of egregious misconduct. Sometimes, the dash cam, a camera
mounted inside the officer's squad car, provides proof of police brutality
and misconduct. Yet, it is the smartphone that has provided the difficult-
to-watch and, for police commands, nearly impossible-to-defend action
of some officers caught on camera doing things that are definitely not in
keeping with standard operating procedures. In 2014, David Diaz used
his cell phone to record the excessive force used by a California Highway
Patrol officer who, when attempting to make an arrest, sat on top of a
woman and beat her about the face and head. The violent footage repeatedly shown by the national news media is for many irrefutable proof of
what has been alleged by members of the black community.

Diaz is one of the more than 300 million Americans who own cell
phones. According to the Pew Research Center, 93 percent of blacks are
cell phone users. In the inner city, the usefulness of the cell phone goes
beyond practicality. In some black communities, and for many blacks in
general, the cell phone's intrinsic value is seen as fundamental to defending one's innocence and/or having to prove the legitimacy of claims of

excessive force and police brutality that would, without digitally recorded evidence, be otherwise dismissed out of hand.

The utilization of technology in both the United States and United Kingdom evolved from 911 and 999, respectively, into the apparatus that law enforcement relies on today, as a principal weapon in its arsenal to combat crime. Surveillance technology when used, especially as it relates to less sophisticated criminal activity, has to an extent proven useful as a crime deterrent. However, the advent and complexity of cybercrime creates an entirely different challenge for law enforcement. Emerging criminal enterprises that prey on the unsuspecting requires that law enforcement organizations keep pace with cybercrime masterminds that have the skill and potential to affect individuals and society overall, in ways that could impact our utilities, water supply, banking industry, and national security. The resources that federal, state, and local law enforcement organizations are required to allocate in order to head off the sinister efforts of tech-savvy criminals is mindboggling, and a burden on taxpayers. However, as Robert Moore, author of *Cybercrime: Investigating High-Technology Computer Crime*, stated: "If there is to be any chance for the criminal justice field to keep pace with those who are using computers and technology to commit criminal acts, then now is the time to begin implementing adequate response plans."[14]

NOTES

1. Joel L. Swerdlow, "Information Revolution," *National Geographic*, October 1995.

2. Victoria M. Walker, "A State Court Says Rap Lyrics Can't Be Used as Evidence in a Criminal Trial," Code Switch, August 6, 2014, http://www.npr.org/blogs/codeswitch/2014/08/06/338303043/a-state-court-says-rap-lyrics-cant-be-used-as-evidence-in-a-criminal-trial (accessed August 11, 2014).

3. "The History of 911 Systems: America's First 911, Haleyville, Alabama," http://www.ecdops.org/history_of_911.htm (accessed January 6, 2014).

4. "9-1-1 Origin and History," http://www.nena.org/?page=911overview facts (accessed January 7, 2014).

5. Emma Murphy, "New Technology for Police Interceptors," *Security Technology News*, August 14, 2013, http://www.security-technology news.com/news/new-technology-for-police-interceptors.html (accessed January 7, 2013).

6. "Cyber Crime," http://www.justice.gov/usao/briefing_room/cc/ (accessed January 7, 2014).

7. Ian Evans, "Report: London No Safer for All Its CCTV Cameras," *Christian Science Monitor*, February 22, 2012, http://www.csmonitor.com/World/Europe/2012/0222/Report-London-no-safer-for-all-its-CCTV-cameras (accessed August 11, 2014).

8. David Barrett, "One Surveillance Camera for Every 11 People in Britain, Says CCTV Survey," *Telegraph* (London), July 10, 2013, http://www.telegraph.co.uk/technology/10172298/One-surveillance-camera-for-every-11-people-in-Britain-says-CCTV-survey.html (accessed January 14, 2014).

9. "Germany and France Call for Talks over US Spying Allegations," October 25, 2013, http://www.dw.de/germany-and-france-call-for-talks-over-us-spying-allegations/a-17182181 (accessed January 6, 2014).

10. Andrew Buchanan, "On Chicago Streets, Cameras Are Watching," *Christian Science Monitor*, July 30, 2003, http://www.csmonitor.com/2003/0730/p01s02-usgn.html (accessed January 6, 2014).

11. Kevin Sheehan, Natasha Velez, and Natalie O'Neill, "Hundreds of Teens Trash Mall in Wild Flash Mob, *New York Post*, December 27, 2013, http://nypost.com/2013/12/27/hundreds-of-teens-trash-mall-in-wild-flash-mob/ (accessed January 7, 2014).

12. Lee Rainie, Pew Research Center, June 6, 2013.

13. Lauren Gambino, *Guardian* (London), July 24, 2014, http://www.theguardian.com (accessed July 26, 2014).

14. Quoted in Ulf Wolf, "Cyber-Crime: Law Enforcement Must Keep Pace with Tech-Savvy Criminals," *Digital Communities*, January 27, 2009, http://www.digitalcommunities.com/articles/Cyber-Crime-Law-Enforcement-Must-Keep-Pace.html?page=2 (accessed August 12, 2014).

9

❖❖❖

Building Confidence
in the Criminal Justice System

"When you have police officers who abuse citizens, you erode
public confidence in law enforcement. That makes the job of
good police officers unsafe."[1]

As U.S. attorney general in 1963, Robert Francis Kennedy, at the pinnacle
of his crusade against organized crime, made this prophetic statement:
"Every society gets the kind of criminal it deserves. What is equally true
is that every community gets the kind of law enforcement it insists on."[2]
It is hard to fathom that a half-century later, the relevance of Kennedy's
words has not only come to fruition, but has done so in ways that could
not have been imagined. In his September 25, 1963, statement to the
Permanent Subcommittee on Investigations of the Senate Government
Operations Committee, Kennedy was mainly focused on the spread of
organized crime in America. However, the attorney general had come to
realize the degree to which elected officials and the criminal justice system
were susceptible to the allure of organized crime. Kennedy also warned
against law enforcement–related issues that confronted contemporary society. Illustrating the sweeping scope of his commitment to preventing the
permeation of organized crime into law enforcement organizations,
Kennedy made reference to an attorney and nightclub operator involved

in organized crime, as well as offered examples of corrupt elected officials and law enforcement officers. In one instance in Newport, Kentucky, the mayor, several city council members, and police officers had been indicted for malfeasance. And in Beaumont, Texas, according to Kennedy, "[s]ince late 1960 when a special squad of IRS agents began intensive investigations there, the wide open vice and corrupt law enforcement which had existed for decades have been largely eliminated"; and, "[a] number of public officials, including the sheriff, district attorney and police chief of Beaumont and Port Arthur each admitted receiving substantial amounts as "political contributions."[3]

Therefore, it is safe to say that Kennedy was acutely aware of the existing temptations and growing occurrence of corruption inside the criminal justice system, and that the potential was present at the highest levels of the law enforcement. However, the fact is that the attorney general's stand against organized crime greatly exceeded local efforts aimed at law enforcement officials that, through their affiliation with the criminal element, were severely tainting the reputation of the majority of respected law enforcement personnel. One wonders if Kennedy's 1963 initiative to reel in police corruption would have been more aggressive as it relates to wayward law enforcement personnel, if it would have helped to curtail the spread of police corruption that was metastasizing like a cancer. Arguably, if the focus had been widened to include what was occurring inside police departments like the NYPD, LAPD, and others where police misconduct was well on its way to becoming systemic in nature, it is possible that some of the issues that former NYPD officer and whistle-blower Frank Serpico brought to light may have been headed off.

That said, we know that the escalation of organized crime, police corruption, brutality, and general wrongdoing was well on its way to becoming a ubiquitous and contentious issue by the time that the Kennedy waged war against it. Still, giving credit where it is due, as attorney general, Kennedy faced down the thriving criminal element that had by then firmed its grip on many areas of commerce, threatening the foundation of American enterprise and values. When considering that much of the growth related to organized crime occurred prior to the Kennedy administration, it is a given that the inroads made by organized crime had been well established decades earlier, and that the Kennedy administration was playing catch-up. Nonetheless, an unfortunate and lingering consequence is the erosion of the public's confidence in law enforcement, as sectors of the criminal justice system became more susceptible to the enticement of organized crime.

The examination of the issues presented in the preceding chapters aided in disclosing and offering insight into problems that plague contemporary law enforcement agencies as well as in bringing to light the policing techniques that offer hope in reducing incidents of criminal activity, police brutality, and wrongdoing by the men and women who are entrusted to serve and protect the public. Yet, years after Kennedy's war on organized crime, our criminal justice system and rank-and-file police officers on the frontline are confronted with situations that could not have been imagined during the 1960s, and that seem to have caught police commands throughout the country off guard. The outcome is the public's waning confidence and support for what police officers do day to day, and what is perceived by some as a loss of empathy and a disconnect within the entire criminal justice system as it relates to the concerns of a growing number of citizens.

Without beating around the bush, there are those who believe part of the problem is the attitude of some police officers that consider the work that they do as merely a job that provides income, excellent benefits, and a decent pension. This way of thinking is consistent with what a distinguished retired police officer shared with me as we talked about the many ills and the potential remedies that are necessary to repair the relationship between law enforcement and the public, as well as to restore the public confidence in law enforcement personnel. The retired officer's revelation came up while we discussed how the majority of police officers initially perceive their oath and responsibility in a sacred and personal way that exemplifies the reasons that they had become police officers in the first place. I recall being shocked when he told me that a great number of officers are rather quickly jaded by the realities of the occupation that they have chosen. He gave the example of officers who are called to a crime in progress and who deliberately take their time arriving, preferring instead to let the incident play out and thereby reducing the chance that they will have to respond. Given that rampant gun violence in cities such as Chicago, Los Angeles, Philadelphia, and many other urban areas is considered routine, what may be emerging as a prevailing logic by some police officers is, why should they put their lives at risk by rushing to a gun battle and being caught in the crossfire? Moreover, he explained that some police officers who are close to retirement are inclined to think twice before jeopardizing the pension that they've worked so hard to attain. Without a doubt, this type of mindset is not in keeping with the pledge to preserve law and order, and if it is a part of the law enforcement culture, surely it is contributing to the growing chasm between law enforcement and some segments of American society. When coupled with socioeconomic issues that are prevalent in some urban locales, such attitudes have an incredibly negative effect on the ability to make headway toward tackling the perception of racism and police brutality, and are moreover an impediment to regaining faith and trust between the residents of urban communities, law enforcement officers, and the criminal justice system.

Assuming that most citizens allow that police officers are entitled to bear in mind rational concerns about the work that they do and the dangers associated with it, and that they should use their common sense in the face of real and present danger, the public does, however, expect adherence to the oath that the officers took to serve and protect. In urban America, where gang violence, the killing of innocents, open-air drug sales, unemployment, blight, and despair are commonplace, logic and sound reasoning are frequently a study in contrast. In fact, in some instances, the views are so conflicting that there are those who actually consider not only the police, but the entire criminal justice system as enemies of the people and, as was previously stated, just another gang wreaking havoc on an already struggling population.

Having said that, one might consider that it is here, at what seems the most crucial and volatile state of affairs, where the elements of power, politics, and racism could be used to channel mutual respect and understanding. It might well be the best opportunity to undertake an effort to reverse the negative viewpoint and nature of the relationship between police officers and residents of minority communities. Obviously, this is not the magic bullet; and there are many hurdles, and frankly, not all of the problems can be connected to the rap against wayward police officers, or to the alienation toward the criminal justice system. To start, some residents of urban communities, where violence is out of control and concern for safety is key in shaping the way that one lives, there is the prevalent attitude of not getting involved and of minding one's business. This viewpoint is tantamount to the police officer who takes his or her time arriving on the scene of a crime. However, the difference is that when the officer's shift has ended, they are able to, in most cases, head home to a safer environment.

Citizens concerned with their safety and the raging violence in their communities continue to grow more harsh in their thinking about what should be done about the out-of-control, gun-wielding thugs and anarchy besieging some urban neighborhoods. Some, and I include myself, are rethinking the role of police officers and seeing differently what law enforcement and the community are up against. In a July 27, 2014, perspective, I addressed the issue, and based on the feedback received, it is clear that the outrage, frustration, and conflicting views related to a solution to the problem is not in sight. However, while people are not ready to surrender their civil liberties or to put up with abuse by police officers, there are definite signs of universal transformational thinking in the law enforcement community and among the citizenry as it relates to working together to get rid of the gangbangers and gun violence. I wrote in the piece that:

I recently discussed Chicago's out of control violence with my friend and sometimes collaborator Angalia Bianca, an implementation specialist at UIC/CeaseFire Illinois.

I told Bianca that I had hardened in my belief about what should be done to stamp out the gangbanging and carnage in some Chicago neighborhoods, and that middle-of-the-road attitudes do not contribute to a solution.

Like others, my viewpoint has evolved, and I can no longer tolerate stale rhetoric that does not directly aim at the gangbanging thugs pulling the trigger.

Yes, I still believe that there is benefit in early intervention, job training and employment opportunities. However, thugs like those responsible for the murder of 28-year-old Wil Lewis, while he was standing at a bus stop blocks from his Rogers Park home, should be locked up and the key thrown away.

Eric Vaughn is the 31-year-old alleged to have ordered a juvenile gang-banger to shoot a rival gang member. However, he missed his intended target, instead hitting Lewis.

On July 19, within a 12-hour time span, 22 people were wounded by gunfire in Chicago. Sadly, while attending a sleepover and making s'mores, an innocent 11-year-old Shamiya Adams was shot in the head and killed.

Thinking in a dramatically different way, I believe that the priority should be to remove from society the individuals that commit these horrendous acts.

The people like the ones that killed Lewis and Adams are giving Chicago a new moniker. Now, instead of being warmly referred to as the Windy City or Chi-Town, some have taken to calling it Chi-Raq.

Having said that, perhaps airlifting the thugs to war zones where as of April 2014, 6,802 uniformed America's sons and daughters have died, should be on the table.

Bianca has loads of street cred intervening in dangerous situations to reason with gang-bangers and find alternatives to the violence.

True to her nature, Bianca listened and without any hint of judgment responded saying that, "poverty, illegal drugs, lack of stable housing, unemployment, mental health issues and lack of education are all root causes to violence. People make mistakes and they need a second chance."

Of course she is right, however, there are also those that are beyond help and second chances. Now is the time for elected officials to demonstrate their political will, and to make the tough decision to utilize Illinois National Guard troops in Chicago.

I witnessed the aftermath of the 1968 riots and realize that mobilizing the military is an extreme measure. However, 14 killed and 82 wounded over the July 4th weekend meets the criteria for declaring a war zone.

Some black leaders continue to resist using the military, saying that it would result in the violation of civil liberties. Maybe they have forgotten that it was the appeal of Dr. Martin Luther King Jr. in 1957 to President Dwight D. Eisenhower to activate federal troops, in order to protect innocent students from violent segregationists in Little Rock, Arkansas.

How much longer should we wait, and how many more innocent people have to die before we take action?[4]

The perspective prompted a spirited reaction indicative of the mounting sentiment of law-abiding citizens who are fed up with the violence and killing of innocent people. An increasing number of people believe that if the law enforcement community and urban residents are able to recognize the frustration as an opportunity to work together in an attempt to quash the violence, it could signify real hope toward strengthening the trust and confidence that minorities and the economically disadvantaged have in police officers and vice versa. However, in order for this to happen, law enforcement organizations and the people must interact in an entirely different way. It is necessary to reset the paradigm and to incorporate a genuine mutual respect, fairness, and a partnership with the public that has previously been considered off limits. For instance, an openness and full disclosure in a city like Chicago would go a long way to help confront the past deeds perpetrated by the evil cabal that ruled for decades under the command of disgraced former CPD commander Jon Burge.

The reality is that the dirty cop is something of an oxymoron. As mentioned in Chapter 4, it is a lot like the question of what came first, the chicken or the egg. Still, it is something that law enforcement organizations must contend with by using a variety of techniques to better filter potential police recruits that exhibit a preponderance for wrongdoing. In addition to improving the scrutiny of possible recruits, there is a need to find and to purge the system of those that have already taken the oath to serve and protect; however, this presents an entirely different set of circumstances and an extremely arduous dynamic.

Nationwide, as police departments endeavor to eliminate corrupt police officers, and organizations like the American Civil Liberties Union, Citizens Oversight Committee in Law Enforcement, and Accountable Authority.com police the police, it is clear that something has to give. For instance, AccountableAuthority.com was formed out of necessity to serve as whistle-blowers and to alert law enforcement commands about police officers and other public servants that they identify as corrupt. The organization defines its mission as being mandatory: "To keep a publicly accessible record of complaints against officers to create a solid foundation for their dismissal from public office, release of false charges against their victims, and criminal and civil prosecution against them."[5]

In urban America, and chiefly in poor minority communities besieged by violence, community watch organizations are fundamental in helping to identify abusive behavior by police officers. Regrettably, when it comes to naming the gangbangers and violent offenders who have turned their neighborhoods into war zones, people don't have the same zeal, and many are reluctant to come forward. As it relates to sensational cases like the wrongful conviction of the Central Park Five, and numerous other highly publicized and controversial cases, the public's outcry has resulted in the establishment of organizations whose primary purpose is to keep an eye on police officers.

For example, the Police Accountability Act defines those bound by it as any "Officer or servant include all officers, employees, agents, contractors and elected officials of any government agency."[6] As proposed, the Police Accountability Act calls for a strict adherence by:

Any officer convicted of a criminal charge or found liable of a civil assessment calculated statutorily based on acts committed while on duty and not addressed in this bill, shall as a result have the penalty or civil assessment automatically doubled.

Any officer preventing a citizens free exercise of rights— constitutionally protected or otherwise recognized by the [D]eclaration of [I]ndependence—shall be discharged from his duty permanently without pay or compensation and shall not be hired again by any law enforcement, private security or take any public office.

An officer violating the civil rights of a person or ordering another officer to violate the civil rights of a person may be held liable for civil damages withstanding sovereign immunity including but not limited to property damage, compensatory damages and punitive damages.

All officers when engaged in duty where their identity is concealed such as a mask or removal of their name from their uniform must wear an identifying number where each digit is at least 2 inches in height on both the front and back of their uniform.

Any officer attempting to block the view of a person[']s video camera, instruct a person to turn off their camera or tell them that they are not allowed to record, attempt to confiscate a camera, attempt to delete recordings from a camera will be a civil rights violation of the [First] [A]mendment. If any physical force or threat is used to in these attempts, the officer has committed a felony assault.

An officer following orders which violate the civil rights of a person shall be no excuse for acting on such illegal orders. An officer refusing to follow these orders shall be protected under the same safeties of whistleblower laws and has the obligation to notify the ordering officer that such orders are illegal and must report such illegal orders to internal affairs. Knowing but refused to report a violation shall be considered conspiracy in the violation and the officer becomes equally liable.

Any officer refusing to identify himself when requested by any person and when reasonable able to do so either verbally or by showing a badge or ID shall be guilty of a misdemeanor and shall pay an amount of $500 to each person for each time they request and the servant refuses to identify himself. If asked to identify himself he must state at the very least his badge number, last name, and office of employment.

If a person is arrested and no charges are filed, the arresting officer shall be guilty of a wrongful arrest and must personally pay an amount of $500 per calendar day that the person spends any time in jail, including time spent in jail after the period bail is granted by the defendant is unable or unwilling to post bail.

If a person if charged by an officer and found to be not guilty or factually innocent, the defendant shall be entitled to full reimbursement for any costs associated with the arrest including but not limited to towing and impound, vehicle storage.

When a person asks an officer if he is under arrest or if he is free to go, the officer must state that the person is either under arrest or free to go. If the person is being detained, and will be free to go as soon as the officer is done conducting his investigation, he must state his probable cause.

If an officer asks a question or asks for a document or asks to search any part of a person or his property, and the person asks in any way if he is required to comply by law, the officer must answer truthfully or shall pay $1000 to the person for each false statement.

If an officer makes any false statement in a police report, the officer will pay the amount of $1000 for each false statement to each person who the false statement can or has negatively affected.

If a person is stopped by an officer, and asks the officer what he was stopped for, the officer must immediately notify the person of the probable cause if any or the reasonable suspicion. If only a reasonable suspicion exists, the officer must state that he has only reasonable suspicion. If at any time the person refuses to continue the conversation, they may walk away, or run away and that action may not be used as probable cause of guilt of any crime. This supersedes any person's obligations such as identifying himself. If the officer refuses to state probable cause the person does not need to identify himself or comply with any of the officer's orders.

A person being arrested who asks for but is not told what he is being arrested for, or asks to see a warrant but is not provided a warrant at the time of arrest, may assume that he is being falsely arrested and may defend himself as if the officer was not an officer but another citizen. If an officer is alerted of a warrant by radio or other communication without possession of the physical warrant, he must wait with the person until the warrant can be brought to the location where the person is to be arrested. No arrest of physical restraint can not take place until the warrant is present. This grants no authority for a person to use any force in self defense that is not otherwise already available to him by the laws of the jurisdiction where the arrest is taking place.

Penalties for public officials violating these acts are payable to the victim in a civil action in the amount of $5,000 per violation per victim.

No officer or agency may obtain insurance against damages arising from this act.[7]

As posed, the changes enumerated in the proposed Police Accountability Act may come off as unreasonable or unnecessary to some, and especially police officers. However, there is no doubt that modification and consistency in policing procedures are needed, especially given the proliferation of guns, violence, drugs, terrorism, identity theft, and other criminal activities that utilize new technologies, and the reality is that some police officers have been involved in the aforementioned criminal activities. In spite of the fact that the recommendations proposed in the Police Accountability Act do not appear to usurp the authority of police officers or to constrain their ability to carry out their sworn duty to serve and protect the public, I say with a fair amount of certainty that police commands, criminal justice professionals, and politicians are likely to perceive the act as being extreme, and that few are likely to embrace it. Moreover, the generally sacrosanct brashness that prevails inside many law enforcement organizations will continue to be a major obstacle to keeping police officers honest, garnering the public trust, and changing the perception of police officers in urban America.

For instance, according to the *Chicago Tribune*, independent journalist Jamie Kalven took on the city of Chicago in an epic seven-year battle to obtain, under the Freedom of Information Act (FOIA), the investigative files related to five Chicago police officers accused of sexually and physically abusing a public housing resident. In spite of the fact that an Illinois appellate court twice ruled that Kalven's request should be granted and that as early as 2007, U.S. District judge Joan Leflow asserted that the public has, "a significant interest in monitoring the conduct of its police officers and a right to know how allegations of misconduct are being investigated and handled,"[8] the city of Chicago and the CPD continued its refusal to release the records. It instead opted to dig in its heels and to spend more taxpayer dollars arguing against turning over files related to a number of police misconduct cases. Possibly realizing that by dragging the matter out would only add to the deep-seated suspicion associated with what Mayor Rahm Emanuel referred to as a, "dark chapter" in Chicago's history, the city ultimately reversed its decision. Chicago Corporation counsel Steve Patton talked about the city's surprising turnaround: "The city of Chicago had the option to continue to litigate this matter, but ultimately we concluded that—with proper safeguards in place—it will serve a greater public good to allow these investigations to be subject to open records laws."[9] The turnabout is significant because it has always been the case that when, after investigating, an alleged act of misconduct by a police officer is deemed factual, the public was able to ascertain the outcome. However, with the Illinois Appellate Court's 2014 ruling, even if the investigative findings are determined to be unfounded, the records must be made available under FOIA. That said, an official record identifying police officers whose names are repeatedly mentioned as it relates to allegations of abusive or criminal behavior will no longer be kept from the public.

The avalanche of complaints against police officers inside law enforcement organizations throughout the country, and the citizenry's demand that police misconduct files alleging the use of excessive force and other infractions, may ultimately benefit the relationship between the public and police, as well as root out officers that engage in unsavory conduct. Because law enforcement organizations are under extreme pressure to find ways to change a culture and, unless forced to do so, will conceal the names and specific allegations against police officers, the outcome of Kalven's arduous seven-year fight could be a game changer. There are numerous examples to illustrate that this is likely—for instance, because of the ruling, *Chicago Tribune* reporters Jeremy Gorner and Annie Sweeney discovered that a list of eight Chicago police officers, said to be the most complained-against by citizens, had been kept from the public for eight years. In their July 31, 2014, story it was revealed that, "Not surprisingly, the most complained-against officers on the list came from one of the most-scandal plagued units in the city's history, the Special Operations Section, an elite unit of officers who in the early 2000s were tasked with taking guns and drugs off the street."[10]

The irony doesn't end there, because some police officers that are alleged to have histories of excessive force and troubled pasts, were, according to the *Chicago Tribune*, hired to teach citizens how to carry firearms under Illinois's conceal-and-carry law. University of Chicago law professor Dr. Craig Futterman, who has studied police brutality, put the alarming contradiction in context: "To allow police officers with excessive force in their career histories to teach civilians about the use of force is 'crazy.'"[11] Minimally, hiring police officers with a checkered past to perform this important function is a perpetuation of the problem and flies in the face of reason, and those working to improve relations between the police and communities. Moreover, the potential for tragedy is clear, and, as Cook County sheriff Tom Dart put it, "Those are the last folks you'd want to hold out as trainers . . . People's lives are at stake."[12]

CITIZEN INVOLVEMENT

It is as Sir Robert Peel said in connection with his Nine Principles of Policing that: "The police are the public and the public are the police; the police being only members of the public who are paid to give full time attention to duties which are incumbent on every citizen in the interests of community welfare and existence."[13]

Not much has been said about the responsibility of citizens and what they can do to improve relations with law enforcement. So there remains the question and lack of clarity regarding exactly how and what, for instance, the citizens of Chicago—or, for that matter, the people everywhere—can do to better the relationship with, and to grow trust in, police officers and the criminal justice system. This is particularly necessary in the face of such a strong opposition to openness, inclusiveness, and the sharing of information by law enforcement organizations, in spite of the frequency of reports of wrongdoing by police officers. Add to that the fact that the punishment doled out to police officers is rather rare, and the opinion of those strongly advocating for greater accountability becomes more persuasive. If poor relations with police are to be improved, citizens must take part and be willing to become proactive in developing an open line of communication with law enforcement agencies. Moreover, they must be prepared to concede that not all police officers are biased in their thinking, and to refrain from faulting every police officer for the misdeeds of some.

Recognized as among the more effective and proven strategies to improve communication between law enforcement and communities are community-policing initiatives. In one example in the 1990s, the NYPD began its community-relations program by instituting a variety of strategies to help combat and more effectively deal with racial tension, often viewed as a major contributing factor impeding citizen and police relations. The NYPD articulated the purpose of its community policing strategy by asserting that, "[t]he goal of community policing is for community residents and police to work together, cooperatively addressing crime in the neighborhood. . . . Through effective police-community relations, community members learn about policing and how to prevent crime, and a police department can learn about neighborhood members and their policing needs. Community policing allows a police department and neighborhood residents to come together to combat crime. The lack of a community policing effort can doom the relations between the police and the community that it is designed to protect."[14]

The NYPD description is certainly made up of the elements necessary to nurture an environment wherein citizens and law enforcement personnel can find common ground, and to work toward reducing crime. However, it very quickly becomes no more than a pipe dream when the parties don't come together to make it happen or are unwilling to comprise. An example of what some believe represents a monumental failure in community policing is seen in Chicago's Alternative Policing Strategy (CAPS) program. Defined at its inception in 1993 as a partnership between the police and community, CAPS became part of Chicago's law enforcement crime-fighting arsenal and was implemented in five police districts by Chicago's first Hispanic superintendent, Matt L. Rodriguez. For a time, CAPS served as a model to other police departments nationwide; over two decades later, the premise that while "police officers continue to enforce the law and respond rapidly to serious crimes and life-threatening emergencies. . . . CAPS recognizes that the police alone cannot solve the City's crime problems. It takes a combined effort of police, community, and City government working together."[15] Fundamentally sound, by most accounts; however, CAPS did not perform as intended.

The breakdown is multifaceted, and the fault is shared by numerous entities, including the police, the public, and politicians. In 2012, incoming Chicago superintendent Garry McCarthy dismantled the CAPS program, opting to replace it with what was termed a "revitalized" approach to Chicago's community policing effort. Superintendent McCarthy's idea was to replace the program that had, in the opinion of some, run its course, with more beat police officers, resident watch groups, and a taking back, through the combined effort of residents' watch groups, police, and individual residents, of streets ravaged by gangs and violence. In a city of 13,500 police officers, neither CAPS nor McCarthy's strategies have, so far, achieved the desired results. So, the question becomes, why after reallocating police officers and moving hundreds from desk jobs to patrol the streets have efforts failed, some say miserably? It is a complex question that can in part be answered with four words, "The No Snitching Rule." Yet, as simplistic as this sounds, it is central to what are a myriad of multilayered socioeconomic and racially sensitive issues confronting modern society, none of which can be easily resolved. Still, unemployment, lack of training, underperforming schools, and an absence of role models are certainly contributing factors. There is the possibility that it is a combination of all these things and more. It is also an enigma that has at its core generation on generation of self-hatred, despair, and isolation for a segment of the population. Superintendent McCarthy may have had a point when he told a Chicago alderman that, "There's no studies that show that more cops means less murders."[16] Yes, it is a great sound bite, but it is also a flagrant simplification of what is destroying entire inner-city communities, and it typifies what the rhetoric has sunk to, while doing little to improve the strained relationship between police and the black community.

However, the distrust between black males and law enforcement persists in black enclaves throughout urban America. Even while this chapter comes to a close, an African American Chicago police commander was accused and charged with putting a gun in a the mouth of a black suspect. According to the *Chicago Tribune*, Chicago Police superintendent Garry McCarthy, who had previously supported Commander Glenn Evans, released a statement: "The alleged actions, if true, are unacceptable to both the residents we serve and to the men and women of the department. As soon as we were made aware of the charges, Cmdr. Evans was relieved of his police powers, pending the outcome of this matter. Like any private citizen, the commander is innocent until proven guilty, and we need to allow this case to proceed like any other. We will cooperate fully with prosecutors."[17]

The history of police corruption tells us something about how we got where we are today, about the role that power politics and racism play in the strained relationship between blacks and the criminal justice system. However, the question of what makes a dirty cop more likely boils down to individual circumstance, attributes, and ethical fortitude. Whether political pressure creates an environment that promotes police brutality and also results in law enforcement organizations making examples of one of their own in order to prove to the public that they are willing to clean house is debatable. However, what is clear and reflected in the number of ongoing DOJ investigations is that there is concern over police corruption at the highest levels of our government. Coming at a time when, because of technological advances, criminal activity is global, it is imperative that federal, state, and local law enforcement agencies genuinely initiate efforts to incorporate transparency, and authentic collaboration with the people.

Case in point: in August 2014, when unarmed 18-year-old Michael Brown was shot and killed by Ferguson, Missouri, police officer Darren Wilson, the incident prompted protests, civil unrest, looting, and ultimately a mandatory curfew and activation of Missouri's National Guard. Images of the civil unrest, militarization of police officers, and incidents of severe treatment of protesters by police, supports the veracity of claims of excessive force, alleged by blacks for decades. The Ferguson incident and its aftermath have focused attention on the chasm between young black males and police across the country, as well as on the divide that includes the entire criminal justice system.

Tense protests, exasperation, and racially explosive situations related deaths of the unarmed black males such as Michael Brown, Trayvon Martin, and Eric Garner have become a catalyst to examine the treatment of black males by law enforcement organizations and others that simmer in urban communities across the country. The volatile situations are complicated by race-powered politics and kneejerk reactions by state, federal, and local law enforcement organizations.

Following the shooting death of Michael Brown and during the civil unrest, I wrote this perspective about the incident:

> If we are serious about dealing in truth, I mean really ready, then let's start by acknowledging that black males are regarded by some as pariahs, and based on the color of their skin that they are regarded as criminals. Yes, it's a tough discussion, but having it opens the door to a meaningful exchange.
>
> Another truth is that some members of the black community through their action, and inaction regarding black on black crime, help to support negative stereotypes. Without a doubt, the shooting death of a nine-year old black boy on the south side of Chicago is proof that something is terribly wrong.
>
> While it may sound like an over-simplification, I wonder if epidemic black-on-black violence, and the killing of innocents have given the false impression that black people devalue human life?
>
> The saying that, "you show people how you want to be treated," comes to mind.
>
> For example, I recently revealed my surprise when learning that excessive force and brutality by black police officers, alleged by blacks, is on the rise. However, it comes as no surprise that the same does not hold true with respect to allegations of excessive force and mistreatment alleged by white citizens, against black police officers.
>
> There is no need to read between the lines, because I am going to say straight out that black police officers think twice about how they approach and treat white criminal suspects. Furthermore, this is not due to mandatory departmental diversity training, or reminders from police hierarchies. It boils down to the fact that the expectation of whites, regarding their treatment by law enforcement personnel is well established and fairly consistent.
>
> Equally sad, is that black males having no gang affiliation, criminal record or history of harming others wake up everyday knowing that they could be the next Mike Brown.[18]

Some believe that the killing of unarmed teenager Mike Brown and the events in Ferguson, Missouri, have ignited a new civil rights movement. If true, it is far and away from the 1960s struggle for equality lead by Dr. Martin Luther King Jr. People of my generation typically think of Rosa

Parks, the mother of the civil rights movement, as the catalyst and icon of the struggle. Also, martyrs like Emmett Till, Medgar Evers, James Chaney, Andrew Goodman, Michael Schwerner and Malcolm X, activists killed during the civil rights movement, are symbols of the struggle. While I wholeheartedly agree that the inequitable treatment by law enforcement and the criminal justice system of young black males is an compelling reason for a new or substantially transformed civil rights movement suited for contemporary society, while indeed tragic and highly suspicious, Brown's death, because of apparent ambiguities, on its own not appear to be ideally suited for that purpose.

Having said that, if Brown's killing by Ferguson police officer Darren Wilson lends the momentum for a new civil rights movement, it has the backing by of an Amnesty International report related to the circumstance of Brown's death that concluded, "Irrespective of whether there was some sort of physical confrontation between Michael Brown and the police officer, Michael Brown was unarmed and thus unlikely to have presented a serious threat to the life of the police officer."

What is clear is that Brown's death has galvanized blacks and advocates of equality, bringing attention to the disparate treatment of black males by some members of law enforcement, as well as the inequitable treatment of blacks by the criminal justice system. In Ferguson and other urban centers a rebirth of a civil rights movement that had until recently woefully lost its way is on the verge of a modern-day resurgence.

In fact, the events in Ferguson and the various factions involved, brings to mind the splintering of Dr. King's civil rights movement, when Stokely Carmichael, a former King follower, became impatient with the pace of King's nonviolent civil rights crusade. Ultimately breaking with Dr. King, Carmichael rejected the nonviolent approach to an insistence of equality for blacks, asserting the radical declaration of demanding "Black Power Now."

Ferguson a half-century later brings us to another fork in the road. The difference is that the dissemination of information helps to quickly unite people, and to illustrate inequitable treatment by law enforcement officials and the criminal justice system.

The exoneration of neighborhood watch volunteer George Zimmerman in the 2012 shooting death of Florida teenager Trayvon Martin is thought by some as proof that the American criminal justice system is racially biased in its treatment of blacks. Clearly it was a rallying point that galvanized concern in the black community regarding the treatment of black boys and men by white police officers.

However, the tipping point came when after more than three months of deliberation, a Ferguson, Missouri, grand jury reached a decision not to indict white police officer Darren Wilson in the shooting death of unarmed black teenager Mike Brown. The decision ignited violent protests, looting, and the burning of local businesses in the St. Louis suburb. The despicable behavior of some protesters ruined what others had hoped to use as an opportunity to peacefully express their dissatisfaction and to demand change. While the chaos resembled something taking place in a war-torn faraway land, the explosiveness showed the level of frustration, and that a segment of the population view the police as the enemy.

Brown's death and the acquittal of the white police officer who killed him marked a turning point in bringing attention to cases where unarmed black males were killed by white police officers without criminal charges being brought against them. The grand jury decision was viewed as a sham and prompted Americans of every race and creed to demand equal treatment under the law for all people.

In the weeks after the Ferguson grand jury decision, another case received worldwide attention, including that of the United Nations. The July 17, 2014, chokehold killing of New Yorker Eric Garner by NYPD police officer Daniel Pantaleo occurred when several NYPD officers attempted to arrest the 350-pound black man for selling untaxed cigarettes. Approaching Garner from behind, Officer Pantaleo placed Garner in a chokehold banned by the NYPD. In spite of Garner's repeated pleas and complaints that he was unable to breathe, the police officers continued to aggressively restrain the 43-year-old father, and Garner died.

Because the entire incident was videotaped with the cellphone of an onlooker, and ruled a homicide by the medical examiner, many were convinced that an indictment against Officer Pantaleo was inevitable. However, when a Staten Island grand jury failed to indict Pantaleo, the outrage was immediate. From coast to coast, urban centers were rocked by mostly nonviolent protests and civil unrest. Americans of every race and creed took to the streets demanding justice for Garner and other victims of overzealous police officers.

In the weeks following the Staten Island grand jury decision, the long-espoused belief that some police officers do not value the lives of black people, especially black males, became the rallying cry.

Within the span of several months, the deaths of Michael Brown, Eric Garner, and Tamir Rice, a 12-year-old black boy killed by a white Cleveland police officer while playing with a toy gun, focused attention on racial profiling, police overreaction, use of excessive force, and the killing of black males by the police. Aside from triggering nationwide civil disobedience, the killings also helped to stimulate efforts to move the investigations of police officers involved in shootings from the local prosecutors, who have a relationship with police that they are investigating, to an independent panel for review and adjudication.

As I close this book, a Cleveland medical examiner has ruled Tamir Rice's death a homicide. Tamir's killing could be another flashpoint in a movement that is exposing racially biased treatment, anxiety, and the widening gulf between blacks and the criminal justice system. To my way of thinking, these are all consequences of wayward police officers, insensitive law enforcement organizations, and inherent biases of our criminal justice system.

NOTES

1. Mary Frances Berry, quoted in "Inspirational Quotes and Quotations about Life in the Law Enforcement Profession, http://www.success degrees.com/inspirational-quotes-and-quotations-on-law-enforcement.html (accessed August 4, 2014).

2. Robert F. Kennedy, quoted in "Inspirational Quotes and Quotations about Life in the Law Enforcement Profession, http://www.success degrees.com/inspirational-quotes-and-quotations-on-law-enforcement.html (accessed July 25, 2014).

3. http://www.justice.gov/sites/default/files/ag/legacy/2011/01/20/09-25 -1963.pdf (accessed October 31, 2014).

4. Anthony Stanford, "Solutions Needed to Stop the Violence," *Beacon-News*, July 25, 2014, http://beaconnews.suntimes.com/2014/07/25/ solutions-needed-stop-violence/ (accessed July 28, 2014).

5. AccountableAuthority.com, https://secure.accountableauthority .com/index.html (accessed July 29, 2014).

6. https://secure.accountableauthority.com/Proposed_police_accountability _act.htm (accessed July 29, 2014).

7. Ibid.

8. Editorial, *Chicago Tribune*, March 24, 2014.

9. Jeremy Gorner and Annie Sweeney, "Cops in SOS Unit Amassed Citizen Complaints," *Chicago Tribune*, July 31, 2014 http://www .chicagotribune.com/news/ct-chicago-police-complaints-met-20140731 -story.html#page=1 (accessed August 1, 2014).

10. Ibid.

11. Dan Hinkel, *Chicago Tribune*, August 7, 2014.

12. Ibid.

13. Sir Robert Peel, quoted in "Inspirational Quotes and Quotations about Life in the Law Enforcement Profession, http://www.success

degrees.com/inspirational-quotes-and-quotations-on-law-enforcement.html (accessed August 4, 2014).

14. *Police Practices and Civil Rights in New York City*, chap. 3, "Police-Community Relations," http://www.usccr.gov/pubs/nypolice/ch3.htm (accessed August 5, 2014).

15. Chicago Police website, "What Is CAPS?" https://portal .chicagopolice.org/portal/page/portal/ClearPath/Get+Involved/How +CAPS+works/What+is+CAPS (accessed August 7, 2014).

16. Mick Dumke, "Superintendent McCarthy Dismantles CAPS, Will Replace It with Something at Some Point," *Chicago Reader*, October 26, 2012 http://www.chicagoreader.com/Bleader/archives/2012/10/26/ superintendent-mccarthy-dismantles-caps-will-replace-it-with-something -at-some-point (accessed August 7, 2014).

17. Jeremy Gorner, *Chicago Tribune*, August 28, 2014.

18. Anthony Stanford, *Beacon-News*, August 24, 2014.

Index

About the Author

Anthony Stanford is a freelance writer and Sun-Times Media Group journalist in the Chicago, Illinois, area. His published works include *Homophobia in the Black Church: How Faith, Politics and Fear Divide the Black Community*, published by Praeger in 2013, and *Revaluing the Federal Workforce: Defending America's Civil Servants*, published by Praeger in 2014, as well as cutting-edge perspectives on politics, race, and religion in the *Chicago Tribune*, such as "Race as a Burning Issue" and "On a Day of Rebirth, Grieving a Loss of Faith." Stanford continues to give presentations related to his first Praeger book, and in 2014, he was invited to present the book to San Francisco Library patrons and to students and faculty at Governors State University. He was named the 2014 Outstanding African-American of the Year by the African-American Heritage Advisory Board of Aurora, Illinois.